MW01094018

SLAYERS

EVERY ONE OF US

SLAYERS

EVERY ONE OF US

HOW ONE GIRL IN ALL THE WORLD SHOWED US HOW TO HOLD ON

KRISTIN RUSSO AND JENNY OWEN YOUNGS

ST. MARTIN'S PRESS
NEW YORK

First published in the United States by St. Martin's Press, an imprint of
St. Martin's Publishing Group

www.stmartins.com

Illustrations by Jenny Owen Youngs

The Library of Congress Cataloging-in-Publication Data is available
upon request.

ISBN 978-1-250-28624-6 (hardcover)
ISBN 978-1-250-28625-3 (ebook)

Our books may be purchased in bulk for promotional, educational, or
business use. Please contact your local bookseller or the Macmillan
Corporate and Premium Sales Department at 1-800-221-7945, extension
5442, or by email at MacmillanSpecialMarkets@macmillan.com.

First Edition: 2025

10 9 8 7 6 5 4 3 2 1

For Buffy Summers, her Scoobies, and ours

contents

prologue

WELCOME TO THE HELLMOUTH

The floorboards in our one-bedroom apartment were massive, wide planks of honey-colored wood original to the brownstone, which had been built alongside Brooklyn's historic Green-Wood Cemetery in 1910. The kitchen was small (when you opened the oven door it nearly touched the opposite wall) and we had only one closet—especially complicated given the fact that we needed room for two people, one cat, and Jenny's fourteen guitars—but it was a magical space frequented by fire escape raccoons and a colony of parakeets that had been roosting in the neighborhood since the 1970s. Local lore maintained that a truck full of green monk parakeets had crashed on its way to a pet store and the birds, once liberated, took up residence in the cemetery's many trees and spires.

The apartment felt so magical, in fact, that Kristin—always waiting for the other shoe to drop—was convinced she'd be hit by a bus for the first four months that we lived there.

"You aren't going to get hit by a bus."

(Jenny has always been a bit more grounded in reality.)

It was 2012, we'd been dating for three years, and things between us had become serious enough for Jenny to cohabitate with Kristin and her aging cat, Trey, despite significant feline allergies. So it was no surprise when, in exchange for this sacrifice, an ultimatum was introduced. For the partnership to stand, Kristin had to do what countless queer women had done before her: she had to watch *Buffy the Vampire Slayer* with her girlfriend.

"It's a show about a *girl* who *kills* vampires but also *dates them* sometimes!"

Jenny, encouraged by the slightest raise in Kristin's eyebrows, continued, "It's also the story of a group of individuals brought together by friendship and fate led by a preternaturally powerful young woman with a sacred calling, waging war against the forces of darkness, sometimes triumphant, sometimes bruised and bloodied by a battle with no end in sight, but one which they cannot give up on, no matter the cost!"

Kristin, not well versed in genre television and always instinctively opposed to a dramatic sales pitch, rolled her eyes. This was not Jenny's first "watch *Buffy* with me" blitz. If anything, she'd lost ground.

"Okay, okay, okay, consider this: it's gayer than you are."

Only then did Kristin take Jenny's DVD boxed set of all seven seasons of *Buffy* off the bookshelf and pick up the remote control.

"Nothing," Kristin said, "is gayer than I am."

And so, we watched.

We'd watched television together before, of course, but watching *Buffy* in this enchanted, cemetery-adjacent, first-home-together space—Kristin sprawled across our IKEA couch with Trey perched on the cushions behind her, Jenny in her favorite spot on the living room floor with a pillow tucked under her head—this was different. If it wasn't already apparent from her displayed boxed set of the series, this was Jenny's *show*. It was a show she'd watched over and over again, anytime she needed comfort, a cozy vampire blanket that had been with her for over a decade. So sharing it with Kristin was no small thing.

Jenny, to her delight, was correct: once Kristin's initial skepticism began to fade, she fell in love with the characters and the story. She laughed when Buffy's mom lovingly made a cup of hot cocoa for the evil vampire Spike, and she cried when Buffy sacrificed her first love in order to save the world. For what it's worth, Kristin maintains that she was also right about at least one thing: nothing is gayer than she is.

Once it became clear that we could share not only a love for each other but also a love for the Slayer, we made plans to marry the following year. As you do.

Our wedding was held at The Bell House in Brooklyn on August 25, 2013. Only two months earlier, we'd held our breath as the Supreme Court decided whether our marriage would be worthy of recognition and protection across the country. It was equal parts powerful and overwhelming when nine appointed justices decided that yes, it was.[1]

The Bell House was a music venue where Jenny had played on many occasions, and it felt like an extension of home. Huge exposed beams crossed the vaulted ceilings in a warehouse space that was built in 1931 and had spent most of its life as a printing press. Our friends and family danced together, ate barbecue fresh from a smoker set up on the sidewalk, and took turns in the venue's vintage photo booth. It was an absolutely beautiful day.

We remained in the brownstone with the wide floorboards for two more years before Jenny's music career took us west.

---

1 In addition to having our marriage recognized on a federal level, we were also delighted to discover that the bakery making our wedding cupcakes offered a 10 percent "same-sex discount."

After years of making albums of her own and touring on repeat, she had the opportunity to explore the world of cowriting
in collaboration with other artists and songwriters, and much
of that world is headquartered in Los Angeles. If our Brooklyn
floorboards could talk, they'd tell tales of Trey's ongoing rivalry
with the fire escape raccoons, his holiday tradition of shitting
under the Christmas tree (just once per calendar year), and his
love of meticulously licking the condensation off of each and
every window during the winter months. They would also have
to tell you about Trey's declining kidneys, about the months
we spent administering fluids from an IV bag to help keep him
hydrated and spry, and the day that two loving nurses came to
our home from the veterinarian's office to ease Trey's transition
into the great beyond.

We left the day after Christmas, without sweet Trey, to
drive to California. We'd emptied the entire apartment of all
of our belongings (*Buffy* DVDs thrice Bubble-Wrapped) except for the Christmas tree itself, which Kristin refused to take
down until the moment we walked out the door for the last
time.

Los Angeles felt like a photo negative of what we'd left behind. Where there once were vivid greens, there were now desert browns; instead of a snowy season, we experienced our first
fire season; in place of our fire escape raccoons, we now had
nightly visits from backyard coyotes. We missed home. Perhaps
to distract us from the things we were missing, or maybe even
as a way to reach back toward our old neighborhood cemetery,
Jenny brought up an idea she'd once proposed in our Brooklyn
apartment: Wouldn't it be fun to start a podcast about *Buffy the
Vampire Slayer*?

Kristin, anxious for any distraction from the black widow
spider we'd found in the kitchen earlier in the week, agreed.

Jenny had already put together a home recording studio in our spare bedroom, and she came equipped with a knowledge of both vampires *and* microphones, so our technical foundation was solid. Kristin, despite her status as a *Buffy* novice, had clocked quite a few hours during her teen years reading Anne Rice and wearing custom-molded vampire fangs to school. Both of us had grown up just a few hours outside NYC in the 1990s, wearing JNCO jeans, smoking clove cigarettes, and listening to Nirvana on our Discmans, so we were also tapped into the nostalgia factor.

We released our first episode of *Buffering the Vampire Slayer* on September 14, 2016. We couldn't have imagined that only a few weeks later, we'd have thousands of new listeners.

We also could not have imagined that a presidential candidate would erupt from a real-life Hellmouth just two months later, win control of the country, and steel us and our expanding community for a fight.

That we'd get pregnant after months of trying, only to experience a miscarriage just hours before going onstage for a live podcast recording in Madison, Wisconsin.

That we'd announce a *Buffy* Prom in Los Angeles and then watch in awe as it sold out in less than three minutes. Or that, just a week before that first *Buffy* Prom, Jenny would tell Kristin she was leaving our marriage.

That in the wake of our divorce, we'd somehow manage to continue podcasting together, bracing through some of our darkest times while simultaneously witnessing some of the podcast's highest highs.

That seven years later we'd still be here, each remarried, one of us with a toddler, still talking about *Buffy the Vampire Slayer* from our separate houses (Jenny in Maine and Kristin in upstate New York) with lives both separate and intertwined.

We didn't know any of this when we sat down to record our first episode, Jenny in her office chair monitoring the audio, Kristin in the cozy green armchair just a few feet away.

All we knew then was that we loved Buffy.

That she and her friends would be riding sidecar to our lives for many years to follow, crisis managing by example, would reveal itself over time.

chapter one

IF THE APOCALYPSE COMES, START A PODCAST

Now might be a good time to provide the uninitiated with some foundational *Buffy* knowledge. Dear reader, into every generation a girl is born, imbued with preternatural strength, speed, and agility, and destined to fight evil. Any evil will do, but there's a particular emphasis on vampires. This might be because vampires are more populous than other demons, or because they're especially meddlesome when it comes to the safety of humans. It might also be because vampires are sexy.

The first season of *Buffy* finds our titular Slayer matriculating at Sunnydale High, having been unceremoniously ejected from her previous school in Los Angeles after burning down the gym, which was full of vampires.[1] In Sunnydale, she makes some new friends (Xander and Willow) and frenemies (Cordelia and Harmony), meets a very hot, mysterious, and possibly-not-evil

---

1 Or, according to the official records of the Los Angeles County Department of Education, "asbestos."

vampire (Angel—he's not like other boys!), and is introduced to her Watcher, Rupert Giles.

In Buffy's sophomore year of high school, also known as 1997, there is one particularly gnarly evil afoot in Sunnydale: an extremely ancient vampire known as the Master. This fellow looks like a cross between Nosferatu and a naked mole rat, and after many centuries spent drinking deep of the blood of the living, he has developed a serious case of fruit punch mouth. (Perhaps we should amend our earlier declaration to: *most* vampires are sexy.)

The Master is the first Big Bad that Buffy encounters, and his to-do list will set the tone for all the subsequent Bads she'll meet in seasons to come. It looks a little something like this:

1. Kill Buffy the Vampire Slayer

As Buffy works to learn more about the Master (and how to defeat him), she discovers an ancient prophecy that foretells that the Slayer will face the Master and she will not survive.

At first, she attempts to sidestep the prophecy by quitting her slay job. In one particularly gutting moment, she looks to her Watcher and says, "Giles, I'm sixteen years old. I don't want to die."

But the next day, several students are slaughtered by vampires at Sunnydale High—students Buffy knew, in a room where she and her friends would often hang out themselves. Willow explains to Buffy that their world—the high school, their friends, the things that make up their lives—does not feel like it belongs to them anymore. Buffy responds to this terrifying revelation by doing something that will come to epitomize the heartbeat of her character: she just keeps fighting.

Just keep fighting, just keep fighting
That's what I'm supposed to do
If I just keep fighting, just keep fighting
Maybe I'll believe it too

Jenny

According to Google Maps, the shortest route from Brooklyn to Los Angeles is 2,789 miles. If you don't sleep and you almost never stop to pee, you can make it in four days. The route that Kristin and I took was slightly more winding and scenic at 3,565 miles over eleven days. We'd both driven across the country many times prior—me as a touring musician, and Kristin as a university speaker focusing on LGBTQ issues— but neither of us had ever been to the Grand Canyon, so we made sure that we routed the trip accordingly.

Before we left New York, my father told us the story of an earlier westward journey. In 1955, my grandparents had driven him from Pennsylvania to California to attend the Rose Parade and visit Disneyland, which had opened just six months prior. He was eleven years old at the time, and when the Youngs family automobile pulled up to the yawning maw of the Grand Canyon on Christmas Day, he'd made a snowball right at the edge. This frosty detail wedged itself deeply in my mind, given the fact that we were traveling through the very same spot sixty years later, almost to the day. We did luck into some canyon snow, and I was able to carry out my ancestral duty; it was dry and hard to pack, but I managed to get two handfuls of powder for a photo that I promptly sent to my very proud dad.

Growing up in an unsung corner of New Jersey made up mostly of forests and farms, I could only ever imagine myself living as an adult in New York City. I loved spending time in the woods but longed to be closer to the thrum of music and art and culture and people, and the infinite possibilities that the city held. Once I got my license, I drove in as often as I could: to see concerts at venues ranging in size from The Living Room's original Stanton Street location all the way up to Madison Square Garden; to catch an arthouse movie that wasn't playing anywhere near my hometown; and to visit museums like the Met, MoMA, and my favorite place in the whole city, the American Museum of Natural History. I became an adult in New York. I started my career in New York. I fell in love, got my heart trashed, and drank to forget in New York.

It was the city where I'd started dating Kristin, where she'd first invited me over for Italian takeout and a viewing of the enjoyable—if not exactly *romantic*—Anne Hathaway film *Rachel Getting Married*. Together we made a home, and one million tiny memories: drinking hot buttered rum at our favorite neighborhood bar on a wintry night, stocking up the pantry in preparation for Hurricane Sandy,[2] picnicking on blankets in Prospect Park during the free concert series every summer, getting married (not unlike Rachel herself!), experiencing the 2010 winter storm nicknamed "Snowmageddon" that was so sudden and intense that buses unable to move any farther were

---

2 The elevation of our building made us one of few households to not lose power, allowing us to drink a lot of on-theme Hurricanes.

left stranded diagonally across intersections, and streets and sidewalks remained buried in snow for days.

My life—our life—was in New York. Leaving was scary. Leaving was exciting. Leaving was something I never thought I'd do until we were doing it.

When we rolled into Los Angeles on January 5, 2016, it rained. It rained for a week straight, in a way that it can only rain in the desert. After years of making fun of Angelenos for their precipitation dramatics, we were instantly humbled. The roads, not engineered to slant and slough off rain the way they do in the Northeast, pooled with water; driving was terrifying. We stayed indoors with Kristin's sister, her boyfriend, and their menagerie of pets (totaling two eighty-pound dogs and one cat) while we scoured the internet for a place to live.

The house we found in Altadena was—and I cannot stress this enough—a *house.* After seeing the rental alongside dozens of other hopeful tenants, Kristin wrote a passionate cover letter to accompany our application, explaining to the owners why we'd make the perfect tenants. My natural tendency had always been to assume that absolutely no one would like to rent me a place to live, and that it is actually borderline rude of me to apply (let alone write a letter and expect them to use some of their very valuable minutes upon this earth to read it!). Thankfully, Kristin's default setting is precisely the opposite: the landlords should be thankful to have us!

Later we discovered that the daughter of the owners had, upon learning of Kristin's work with LGBTQ communities, insisted that we be the ones to get the place. Our wedding had been blessed with a queer cupcake discount, and now this?!

The rental was a three-bedroom ranch nestled in the Altadena foothills, with a lemon tree and a baby peach tree in the backyard. Three bedrooms were two more than we'd ever had, and on top of that there was a garage! The space meant that we had a bedroom for ourselves, a guest room to welcome family visiting from the Northeast and friends coming through town, and a proper studio space where I could host songwriting sessions and record music.

Once settled, I doubled down on my efforts to lure Kristin into making a *Buffy* podcast with me. "It will be fun!" I promised. "It won't feel like work, and it will hardly take up any time!" She was wise enough to realize I was dead wrong about my latter claim (though my denial would last years), but the promise of "fun" had gotten its hooks in her. Four months after we moved into our California abode, my music studio also became our shared podcasting space.

At the time, I was listening to podcasts at all hours of the day; I'd go running in the morning with *Death, Sex & Money*, enthusiastically sweep out our new garage with *The X-Files Files*, and shout at Kristin about the most recent *Game of Thrones* facts I had learned from *A Cast of Kings* over dinners of roasted chicken and potatoes. The more hours I spent learning from—and laughing with—these shows, the more I felt a sort of familiar pull. When I first started learning to play guitar in junior high, and began tentatively combining bits of poetry (eek) that I'd been scribbling in my Five Star notebook with chords I'd just learned and melodies I barely knew how to pull together, I experienced an electric surge—half the buzz of creation, half the sensation of reaching toward the thing that inspired me—that made me feel all kinds of feelings. Taking the first step over the threshold into podcast host-hood transferred the same sensation of magic and possibility. I wanted to make a podcast for the same reason I had wanted to make music: because I loved *listening*.

While Kristin hated podcasts (remarkably, this remains

true), as an Italian-born, Long Island–raised triple fire sign, she *was* well practiced at having loud opinions, and brought a masters in gender studies along with a robust history of public speaking to the table. At the jump, we both thought my love of the format and her enthusiasm for soliloquizing would be enough to usher us into the podcasting space with ease. Just as Buffy had once breezed into the hallways of Sunnydale High, excited to start over at a new school free from vampires, we too walked baby-faced into a new city, our new studio, and our brand-new, entirely conquerable careers as podcasters.

Cut to: Buffy encountering an exsanguinated body on campus her first day of school, Kristin tearfully sitting in a corner of the studio after our first recording, and me sighing heavily at my desk as I put down the fourteen pages of notes I'd taken on the series premiere.

After recording our first attempt at a pilot episode and then promptly dragging the file into the computer's trash bin, we realized that this was going to be trickier than we had imagined.

We talked through the difficulties that emerged in our first taping (Kristin's impatience, my attention to detail), and together we vowed to try our best to rein in our individual counterproductive tendencies. A few weeks later, we rewatched the pilot, took new notes, and sat back down in the same studio chairs to record our first episode for a second time. It was better this time around. We felt ready to share it with the world, despite knowing we still had a lot to learn.

I decided that in addition to recording a podcast each week, I would also write an original song from the perspective of Buffy Summers to pair with each episode.[3] If Buffy was beheading a

---

3 Remarkably, even after making this decision, I remained convinced that creating the podcast would take up hardly any time at all!

vampire with a cymbal (hey, it's what was available at the time!), I would sing about it. If a new substitute teacher was seducing teen boys before morphing into a human-sized praying mantis and chomping off their heads, I would try to find the right melody to capture the mood. And, to make things even more complicated, I decided that I would write these songs with Kristin, who (as you may have gathered) was not a musician but (as you also may have gathered) definitely had a lot to say.

In the beginning, Kristin barely knew the difference between a pre-chorus and a bridge.[4] There was a great deal of decoding that needed to occur, with me translating Kristin-speak into musician-speak and then back again. Kristin would say things like, "It just doesn't sound, like, *round* enough to me," leading me to launch a full-scale investigation into what that could possibly mean. Did the vocal need more reverb to soften its edges? Did I need to adjust the EQ of a particular instrument by shaving off some of the high frequencies?? If I applied tape emulation to the master channel, would it add warmth sufficient to appease Kristin's discerning ear?!

If we'd been friends who had just started working together, we probably would have done a better job at drawing boundaries around when to voice our frustrations . . . and when to not. Between the upheaval of a cross-country move and this new, confusing space of sharing work without a shared language, we argued more than usual. Kristin likes to say that I think to talk, and she talks to think; this is a communication incongruence that leaves all kinds of room for conflict.

---

4 She was also a notorious neglecter of lyrics; well into her thirties, she believed the lyrics of a certain massive Joni Mitchell hit to be about paving paradise in order to create a *beautiful* parking lot.

During a recording, I might make a comment that was light on details, assuming she would be able to read between the lines. Kristin, never having met two lines that she cared to read between, would interpret my brevity as a personal slight. I would get annoyed with her for misconstruing my meaning, and she would feel hurt and start crying; I would throw up my hands. This kind of exchange occurred all too frequently and almost always ended in tears (which felt to me like the playing of some kind of emotional trump card, because how can you argue with the tears of someone you love?!). At the start, we'd often have recording sessions together where one or the other of us would get so overwhelmed that we'd have to stop the taping midthought and step out of the studio. Sometimes we would be able to talk it through, and other times we'd get so frustrated that we'd have to shut the whole operation down for the evening and come back to it all over again the next day.

At the same time, we were seeing an incredible response to our first few episodes. We both had large queer networks who sent out their various bat signals ("Alert! Alert! Two queers are talking about *Buffy*!"), and we were featured almost immediately on the iTunes homepage. Before we had even published our third episode, the podcast was included in the *print* edition of *Entertainment Weekly*. *Entertainment Weekly*!!! (May she rest in peace.) We didn't have a stenographer in the room when we found out about this particular milestone, but it's safe to say that our dialogue went something like this:

Kristin: AAAAAaaaaAAAaAAAaaaaaahhh!!!!!
Jenny: HAJSHFJHSDJFHSDLJFHSDJ!!!!!!

I drove to Vroman's Bookstore in Pasadena and bought three copies of the *EW* issue in question.[5] We posted a photo to our social media accounts of me, down on one knee, proudly holding up the page that shows *Buffering* featured in their Must List and grinning from ear to ear.

In Sunnydale, we followed along as Buffy moved to a new town (just like us!), enrolled in a new school, formed a new social circle, and struggled to accept her dual fates as Regular Teen and Chosen Slayer. As Kristin and I navigated the fresh terrain of Southern California, Buffy was trapping the essence of an evil witch inside a cheerleading trophy, reinstating order after her classmates were possessed by hyenas, and discovering that the gorgeous stranger who kept showing up with hot tips for how best to fight vampires was actually (gasp!) a vampire himself. Sure, there were the occasional rumblings that warned of a darkness rising up from below, but Buffy had a perfect record of kicking demon ass in her new town, and we had our shiny new podcast. We'd all be fine!

Kristin

I'm someone who has always instinctively tried to cram the square pegs of chaos into round holes of order. Nearly anything can be made into a tidy list! Spreadsheets are our best friends! If there is a plan, and a backup plan, and a backup plan for the backup plan, then I can be ready for *anything*. In December

---

5 In what would appear to be a special treat from the universe to me, this issue's cover features Grade A hunk Sam Heughan of *Outlander* fame. As *Buffering* continued, my status as the hunk aficionado of the podcast would become cemented, then bronzed, then eventually encased in carbonite.

2015, I desperately wanted my brain, body, and heart to be prepared for a cross-country uprooting. So, before Jenny and I moved to Los Angeles, I obsessively and meticulously packed every room of our Brooklyn apartment, one at a time, and documented each with a photo on Instagram.

> **December 14:** A half-empty bookcase; a few candles and a holiday penguin Jenny made as a child on the top shelf; some graphic novels on the bottom shelf; "The Living Room."
>
> **December 15:** An old tour poster lying on the hardwood floor with a small plastic figurine of Dana Scully; an origami turtle; a pile of pens; "The Office."
>
> **December 16:** Me, kneeling on our bare queen mattress, giving the camera double middle fingers; "The Bedroom."
>
> **December 17:** A paper HAPPY BIRTHDAY banner draped across the doorway; a newly thirty-five-year-old me looking skeptical; "A Brief Respite."
>
> **December 18:** A taped-up cardboard box; the bottom half of my body perched on the tub; one bathmat; one towel; "The Bathroom."
>
> **December 19:** A selfie in one of my favorite shirts at the time—a gray long-sleeve covered in cartoon pizza slices—with dozens of drinking glasses and mugs lining the counter behind me; "The Kitchen."

I was leaving the only city I had ever known as an adult person, and that required bringing outside order to a time that felt, inside, like an earthquake.

When we arrived in Los Angeles, I didn't even have my own car—and LA is famously a *driving* city. In the span of a few weeks, I went from being able to walk out my door and scoop up anything my heart desired within a block or two to being stranded at our house on any day that Jenny took the car to a songwriting session. My first effort at quieting the increasing thrum of isolation inside my chest was to painstakingly *un*pack all our moving boxes. I hung artwork, I unrolled rugs, I tucked clothing back into dresser drawers, and one day I spent five *entire* hours arranging the display on our fireplace mantel. Once the last box was unpacked, I found myself at an impasse. Now what would I do to battle my growing feelings of loneliness and disorientation?

Where even *was* I?

What *was* this place?!

There was never a better time for me to say yes to making a podcast about *Buffy* with Jenny. *Buffy* has 144 episodes in its seven-season run! 144!!! Our Brooklyn apartment and our Altadena house only had thirteen rooms *combined* for me to pack and unpack—this new endeavor would surely carry me through the seas of life upheaval until, I reasoned, everything would settle into place, and I would feel like I was home again.

But 2016 had different plans for us all.

The marrow of *Buffy*'s first season is an impending battle: an ancient evil is prophesied to rise and wreak havoc on the world, and Buffy is tasked with averting an actual apocalypse. As their sophomore year churns forward, Buffy and the Scoobies[6] grow increasingly anxious: What if they cannot win the fight? In our new California home, tension was also mounting as a different kind of evil seemed poised to envelop *our* world. While Buffy braced for impact in Sunnydale, we were anxiously watching the presidential election draw closer and grow

---

6 The canonical name given to Buffy's best friends, who—much like the *Scooby-Doo* squad—spend a great deal of their time foiling evildoers.

uglier with every passing week. As Buffy learned more about the Master and his army, the fractures in our own world were revealing themselves to run deeper than many of us had imagined possible.

On top of my ongoing struggle to find comfort in a new city thousands of miles away from anything I'd ever known, the election was now casting a harsh light on the divide between my beliefs—my existence, even—and the beliefs of my conservative Catholic family.

My mom is one of eight sisters—remarkably, my grandmother had eight girls and not a single boy—and even though I have twenty-five cousins on my mother's side alone, I remain the only out queer person in my entire family. When I first came out to my parents over Thanksgiving dinner in 1998, the news was not received well. In the weeks and months that followed, my mom cried often, and many of my aunts pleaded with me to choose a different path. Leaning into an instinctive (and survivalist) tradition among many queer kids, I learned to tuck certain parts of myself away to keep the peace; I participated in conversations where I could fully be myself and danced around the ones where I could not.

My mom, possibly because she was *my* mom, perhaps because she was married to my very logic-and-reason-based dad—or maybe due to the triple whammy of having a liberal husband, a queer daughter, and a second daughter who was also vocally in support of equality, science, and dinosaurs—came around. By the time Jenny came into my life—eleven years after that fateful Thanksgiving dinner!—my mom was not only comfortable meeting her but also delighted in her presence.

Over the years, Jenny and both of my parents developed relationships that were all their own. Jenny perfected a magnificent impression of my dad's most effusive Italian hand gestures that she'd perform for him on our visits north; my mom learned all Jenny's favorite coffees and would stock up on them before we arrived. My dad would pull Jenny into his office to tell her all about the newest music he was listening to ("Have you heard of Leona Lewis?"). My mom would sit across the kitchen counter and marvel at Jenny's impeccable pancake making.[7]

I had been hopeful that, slow as it may have been moving, progress was also happening in the more distant branches of my family tree.

A year or so into dating, I brought Jenny with me to the house where my mom had grown up—a three-bedroom, one-bathroom house built by my grandfather and his two brothers right across the street from the high school football field.[8] After my grandfather's passing in 1994, one of my aunts moved into the house with her husband and six children, and they constructed an apartment on the first floor for my grand-mother.

The house had always been magical to me, and I was ex-cited to share many of its stories with Jenny. I took her on a full tour, showing her the basement, which housed the laun-dry room (can you *imagine* the amount of laundry?), as well

---

7 My mom still adoringly recounts the first time Jenny made pancakes at their house in upstate New York. In an unfamiliar kitchen, Jenny paused between each step of the pancake-making process: "Rose, where do you keep the *in-sert long Jenny pause* flour?" "Sorry, Rose, where can I find the *pause pause pause* spatulas?" At some point in this back-and-forth, my mom decided it was best to give Jenny a detailed tour of the kitchen, showing her where each thing was kept and explaining that she should treat our kitchen like her own.

8 The three Lang brothers made a perfect construction trio: my grandfather John was a plumber, his brother Bill was a carpenter, and his other brother, Joe, was an electrician.

as my grandfather's old workshop—once full of collapsible yardsticks and rectangular-shaped pencils and even a machine that he used to forge two coins into my parents' wedding rings (a quarter for my dad's and a nickel for my mom's). The supporting beams of the house still had pencil and pen etchings in them from the 1960s and '70s that told tales of the many crushes my aunts had throughout their high school years.

We went out to that Long Island house on many occasions after that first visit, usually staying for dinner with my aunt, uncle, and cousins before riding the LIRR back home to Brooklyn. My uncle was a musician like Jenny (in fact, he was the one to introduce me, at age twelve, to Led Zeppelin and Pink Floyd), and after the dinner plates were cleared, they would sometimes play guitar together for the rest of us. On one of our visits, he and Jenny discussed their shared love of country music, and Jenny told him how she'd found herself unexpectedly bursting into tears when she'd heard Lee Brice's "A Woman Like You" for the first time. The song is sung from Lee's perspective, and he tells the story of his wife asking him what he thinks his life would be like if they'd never met. He details all the fun things he'd likely be doing in her absence, but then goes on to explain that, after all those things, he'd just be out there looking for her.

Several months later, when we went to see my uncle play at a local bar, he paused before beginning his next song and announced to the room, "This song is for my two nieces." When he started singing "A Woman Like You," we were both astounded. He'd meant *us*. He'd dedicated a love song to us—one he remembered had meaning to Jenny—and he'd called us *both* his nieces.

When our wedding invitations went out, we both figured that at least those who'd been in relationships with us would RSVP in the affirmative. We figured wrong. While four of my aunts were in attendance, three were not. That same uncle who dedicated a song to us did not attend. Adding insult to injury, he also asked all six of his children and their families to abstain, and they did. My maternal grandmother (and only living grandparent at the time)—also at the urging of extended family—did not attend.

We were both crushed. And we were both angry.

But it wasn't until the 2016 election that we reached our breaking point. Initially, I feared that *one* of my seven aunts—the most conservative—might vote for our real-life version of the Master, but that the others, guided by their Christian morals, would (at the very least) decline to vote.

When I learned the truth—that seven of those eight sisters (my mother being the only outlier) planned to push for this man's victory—I finally snapped. I pleaded with them. I argued with them. I begged them to reconsider. I explained, again and again, that the choice they were making was diametrically opposed to my health and safety and the health and safety of so many others. I offered personal stories, news articles, facts, figures, maps, anything. Everything. And then, when they did the thing they were always going to do, the thing that now seems so glaringly obvious but then felt like being held underwater, I finally walked away. I stopped engaging in pleasantries over phone calls and text messages. I stopped going to family gatherings.

It was devastating.

Despite all of this, Jenny and I still somehow had hope that the outcome of the election would be what it *had* to be. Soon enough, this unhinged joke would end and we would laugh, wide-eyed, at how *that* almost happened. This was how the story would surely go: Buffy would triumph in her first big battle of the series, and so would we. The Big Bads would be defeated.

On November 8, Jenny and I walked from our little rented house to Altadena's Farnsworth Park and cast our votes.[9]

We all know what came next.

We both decided to skip an election party that night and instead stayed home to work. Jenny was in the studio finishing up the song for our eighth episode, "I Robot, You Jane" (in which Willow is catfished by a demon who has accidentally been scanned out of an ancient tome and uploaded to the internet), and I spent a good portion of the evening on the phone with my increasingly distraught sister. It's reasonable to assume that we had dinner, though no one can say for certain. I had not smoked a cigarette in years, but as the hours wore on, I finally caved and drove to the gas station to buy a pack of American Spirits.

Our constant companion that night was the low hum of election coverage in the living room. Early in our Los Angeles residency, we'd picked up an old 1960s console television set at the local thrift store. The screen was set in a massive wooden case, framed by built-in speakers and drawers that didn't open. It was huge, it was heavy, and we'd had a heck of a time lugging and shoving it into the back of a friend's truck. Mercifully, it came with wheels, which meant that once we hoisted it *down* from the truck bed, we could roll it directly through the front door and into the house. It was via this relic that we

---

9 We were shocked when we recognized this location as the exterior of Xander and Anya's wedding venue in the episode "Hell's Bells." The outcome of that episode is pretty awful, too.

received constant updates as electoral votes were finalized and the outlook grew increasingly grim.

Our podcast episode for "I Robot, You Jane" was scheduled to go live the next morning. Given how entirely upside-down we felt, we considered delaying the episode's release, but ultimately decided against it; maintaining a small semblance of routine and levity felt important, for ourselves and for our listeners. Here we were, in a very dark hour, with the ability to reach out to a new community—one that, from the start, was heavily populated by LGBTQ folks—at a moment when we all seemed to need it most.

Even in the earliest days of podcasting about *Buffy* with Jenny, I felt a deep comfort in the work, the laughter that came with it, and the resulting conversations that we shared with our listeners. After my third or fourth cigarette (a decidedly less healthy comfort), Jenny and I sat down together in the studio at one in the morning to record a message that would play before the episode began. This is what everyone who tuned in on the morning of November 9, 2016, heard:

We know that many of you are feeling scared, sad, and alone. So are we. In response to some of those feelings, we wanted to share a quote from Season 4, Episode 1, "The Freshman": "When it's dark and I'm all alone and I'm scared or freaked out or whatever, I always think, what would Buffy do?"

I think we all know what Buffy would do. She would gather her friends close, and she would fight. And we all know Buffy. We all know her friends. Together, they never stop fighting. Together, they hold each other up. And together, no matter how long it takes, they win. And so will we.

Both of Us

Perhaps, dear reader, you can relate to the feeling of not knowing what to do with your hands; say you enter an unfamiliar environment, or you experience an anxiety spike, and all of a sudden you find yourself wondering, just what *are* these weird wiggly things jutting out from where your wrists end, and where do they go? Into your pockets? Jauntily resting upon your hips? Steepled below your chin as though you might be moments away from tying someone to the train tracks in a silent film?! In the days following the election, we could not for the life of us figure out what to do with our entire *bodies*. We couldn't sit still (except for those moments when sitting still was *all* we could do, while staring bleakly into the middle distance), and buzzed about in an attempt to feel better.

The day after the election, we held an impromptu live stream, broadcasting from our living room to the living rooms (and bedrooms, bathrooms, and beyond-rooms) of hundreds of our *Buffering* listeners. Folks tuned in from all over, huddling around the glow of their screens. Our motive was simple: spend time together, laugh if we could, and let a little light in. Up until this point, our transmissions usually traveled in one direction: our voices through microphones to listeners. In this moment, though, we were able to hear from our audience in real time. We read their comments and questions; we shared our fears; Jenny played music for us all.

The following week we extended that same principle to our social circle, inviting every queer person we knew in Los Angeles to come to our house, eat hamburgers and tofu dogs off the grill, and try to take a little comfort in one another's company (and wine, and s'mores). Fueled by a potent combination of dread and fury, Kristin wrote articles about supporting queer youth for *Bitch* magazine, *Autostraddle,* and *Buzzfeed,* and then flew to Charlotte, North Carolina, to speak in support of trans equality at The Fillmore.

Just a few short weeks and three *Buffy* episodes later, we'd also arrived at the finale of our first season. Watching "Prophecy Girl"—the episode where Buffy has her final battle with the Master—alongside thousands of other *Buffy* fans in such close proximity to the election hit hard. Many of us were experiencing the kind of oxygenlessness that usually results from a swift and stealthy gut punch. It felt like a genuine evil was more tangible, real, and powerful than ever before. The world felt darker and less safe in a way that suddenly had a name and a face. When we talked about the evils of Sunnydale and the movements of the monsters that lived below it, the metaphor gripped us tightly. Similarly, when we watched Buffy and her chosen family hold each other to seek out their strength, we saw our own reality—and communities—reflected.

Up until this point we'd only written songs where Jenny sang as the voice of Buffy, but when we sat down to write the song for "Prophecy Girl," we immediately recognized that the lyrics could come from both Buffy's perspective and our own. This was a moment where we barely had to reach to find the lyrical overlap between the Slayer's experience and *our* emotional state out in the real world.

While Jenny normally wrote music with her guitar in her arms, on this night we sat side by side at the studio desk as she worked to find the right chords on the keyboard. Kristin sipped a whiskey and dug through the episode script for lines of dialogue that would help us unlock the lyrics. Buffy was facing evil, and we were facing evil. Buffy was terrified of what would happen if she lost the battle, and so were we. We shaped the song around that shared sense of fear.

I face nightmares every night
But now I want to run instead
From what will come, what will come
If our world belongs to them

+ ⁺ ⁺ ⁺

"Prophecy Girl" was released on December 7, 2016. Eleven days later, we took the stage at Union Hall in Brooklyn to celebrate our completion of Season 1 with a performance of all the songs we'd written for the podcast up to that point.

It was the first time we had ever witnessed a whole room full of our listeners standing together. Falling just a few weeks after the election and a few days before Christmas, the event was both festive and emotionally charged. Some of our nearest and dearest joined us onstage—wearing Santa hats, singing harmonies, and accompanying Jenny on various instruments (including, of course, many jingle bells).

Kristin debuted what would become our most infamous costume piece: a sixteen-dollar rubber praying mantis mask that she wore while dancing around as Jenny played the song "Teacher's Pet." You might remember us mentioning a substitute teacher at Sunnydale High who was also a giant praying mantis? To expound just a touch: her name was Ms. French, and while in human form she was a total babe, unfortunately in *all* of her forms she was on a mission to mate with as many teenage boys at Sunnydale High as possible, engaging in the time-honored mantis tradition of devouring the head of the male post coitus.

During our performance of the song, Jenny sang (as always) from the perspective of Buffy ("Would you get a fuckin' load of this substitute / Spinning her head around on top of her neck") and Kristin took it upon herself to play the part of Ms. French, so proud of her beheading accomplishments that she must dance the gleeful dance of a triumphant mantis. This bit would remain a staple of our live tapings and performances over the next six years.

We played through the music of our first season chronologically, winding through songs such as "The Pack" (a sixties girl group–inspired bop about that special time in a young girl's life when her BFF is possessed by the spirit of a hyena), "Angel" (in which the heart of the Slayer wants what it wants, regardless of her love interest's very literal body count), and "Prophecy Girl," which closed out the night.

In the final fight between Buffy and the Master, he wins. He holds Buffy's head underwater until she loses consciousness and stops breathing. She dies. It is Xander, a teenage boy with no supernatural abilities, and Angel, a vampire with a soul trying to make amends for the sins of his past, who find Buffy's body. Angel has vampire strength, but no breath (vampires, you see, do not breathe). While Xander does not possess magical powers, he does have air in his lungs. Angel and Xander work together to bring Buffy back to life while, above them, the rest of the Scoobies fight off the monsters being released from the Hellmouth. Buffy—now revived and doubly pissed—finds the Master up on the roof of the high school and, on her second attempt, she kills him.

In New York, the room fell silent as everyone took their

places onstage for the final song. Most of the folks in the audience knew what we were about to play, and it felt like the room held its collective breath as the opening piano chords sounded.

Jenny began singing the first words, and a handful of people in the audience sang along. With every passing lyric, it seemed that more voices were joining in. To our surprise, by the time we reached the chorus, the entire room was singing with us.

> *If I just keep fighting, just keep fighting*
> *maybe I'll believe it too*

Jenny finished singing the second verse, and the audience sang the second chorus even louder.

> *If I just keep fighting, just keep fighting*
> *I think that I'll believe it too*

When we sat down to write the song, we'd made the decision to anchor our message to that final line of the chorus; we felt that was the place where we could try to shine a small light—for ourselves, as well as for our listeners. While in the first iteration Buffy sings, "*maybe* I'll believe it too," by the second chorus she is singing, "*I think* that I'll believe it too."

In early December, we had been writing the song from inside those first two choruses, uncertain that we could ever *really* make it any further. We hoped that by writing it, speaking it, singing it, and repeating it, we could somehow will ourselves into a place of strength.

Union Hall was a sold-out show, so folks were shoulder to shoulder with each other, all singing, some crying. One month after the election, three weeks before the inauguration. Together, we all sang the final chorus:

If I just keep fighting, just keep fighting
I know that I'll believe it too

This was the moment that made us . . . *us.*

What began as two people talking into microphones about our beloved vampire show was changing, morphing, expanding into a community. We were somewhat accidentally becoming a hub, a meeting place, a little beacon to which an increasing number of listeners were finding their way—people who wanted to revel in the collective love of their favorite story, and also find strength in one another. Though our experiences were varied, our fear during that time was something that we all shared. We didn't know what to do, or how to do it, but singing together in that room, we felt—all of us—a sense of purpose, and a certainty that we were not alone.

Once they enter the battle, Buffy and the Scoobies can't control whether they win or lose—they can only choose how to fight: together.

PROPHECY GIRL

Well I heard the words you said
But I can't make them make sense
I face nightmares every night
But now I want to run instead

From what will come, what will come
If our world belongs to them
What will come, what will come

Just keep fighting, just keep fighting
That's what I'm supposed to do
If I just keep fighting, just keep fighting
Maybe I'll believe it too

When you sat there on the bed
Looking scared, looking ahead
Couldn't shake the things you'd seen
And it woke me when you said

What will come, what will come
If our world belongs to them
What will come, what will come

Just keep fighting, just keep fighting
That's what I'm supposed to do
If I just keep fighting, just keep fighting
I think that I'll believe it too

Fire rising in my bones
I can free us from his hold

From the fear that keeps us bound
I am standing, now I know

What will come, what will come
If our world belongs to them
What will come, what will come

Just keep fighting, just keep fighting
That's what I'm supposed to do
If I just keep fighting, just keep fighting
I know that I'll believe it too

Buffering's Own Scoobies

It's important for us to explain early on that, just as *Buffy* refers to the core crew fighting alongside the Slayer as Scoobies, we too refer to the wonderful people who make up the *Buffering* community as *our* Scoobies. Their presence supports our work in every way imaginable, and they hold each other up just as powerfully.

We delighted in the queer ships inside *Buffy* (yes, of course, you've heard of Faith[1] and Buffy, but have you considered Joyce and her book club companion Pat??), and we had chosen families of our own who were woven into our conversations on the podcast. We've often heard from listeners that the act of us simply existing—just being two queer women talking about a vampire show *as queer women*—helped them come out to themselves and to others; that being in *Buffering* spaces, which

---

1 OMG but just in case you haven't: Faith Lehane is, miraculously, *another* Slayer, in stark opposition to the "one girl in all the world" element of Slayer lore. She wears leather pants. She wrestles alligators. She is the bad girl whose mission, apart from slaying vampires, is to encourage Buffy to "find the fun," even if the fun in question happens to be illegal. She is, in the immortal words of Hrishikesh Hirway, both *troubled* and *Trouble*. Lock up your . . . everyone!!!

by extension are mightily queer, helped them feel seen and understood for the first time.

Queerness was only one of many places where our listeners found commonality. Whether they were starting up a new game of Dungeons & Dragons, coming out as trans to family for the first time, getting a mental health diagnosis, or a combination of all three, it seemed that here, in the *Buffering*verse, you could nearly always find someone who *got it*.

One of our favorite online spaces, formed early on in the podcast's run, was intended as a landing pad for emotional solidarity. Scooby Support, as the group came to be known, was a place where you could go to vent about anything and everything, and know that compassionate folks would be there to listen.

Months after its creation, we learned that the group had started a practice of delivering in-person care packages. They would work out who was geographically closest to a Scooby in Need, and then the rest would pitch in financially—a couple

of dollars from some, more from those who had more to give. The person who lived closest would then use the funds to assemble a care package—maybe a book, maybe some cookies, maybe a card or a gift certificate to the local coffee shop—and leave it at the door of the Scooby who was having a rough time. These little tokens of hope would be delivered to folks who had gotten into car accidents, who'd missed a rent payment, who'd decided to leave their long-term partner. Without fanfare, they helped each other stand up again.

One of our other favorite Scooby initiatives was the Siblinghood of the Traveling Yummy Sushi Pajamas. For context, one of Buffy's most celebrated outfits is a set of pajamas, printed all over with a sushi pattern, known, aptly, as her "yummy sushi pajamas." No surprise, then, that one of our listeners acquired a baby onesie (size: newborn) also covered in sushi. When that newborn outgrew the onesie, a post went up on the *Buffering* Facebook group asking if anyone else was expecting. This kicked off what has become a yearslong tradition of the "yummy sushi onesie" being mailed from one family to the next. Listeners post photos of the newest members of the *Buffering* family wearing the onesie, then pass it along to the next person on the list.

If you look at nothing else, do yourself a favor and find the photo at the center of this book showcasing some of those teeny, tiny Scoobies.

chapter two

CLOSE YOUR EYES

In Sunnydale circa 1997, it seems everyone is falling in love. Buffy's best friend Xander is dating classic high school "mean girl" Cordelia. Giles is romancing Jenny Calendar, another faculty member whose technopagan practices conflict with his more Luddite leanings. Buffy's *other* best friend Willow is smitten with a very nice boy (never you mind that he also happens to be a werewolf). Evenings are divided between homework, patrolling area cemeteries for the evil undead, and dancing at Sunnydale's local teen hotspot, the Bronze.

Buffy is *also* falling in love with her tall, dark, brooding, and conveniently ensouled vampire boyfriend, Angel.[1] After his soul was restored, Angel spent the next century repentantly feeding off rats in alleyways and generally looking a mess. Thankfully, by Buffy's sophomore year he has gotten it

---

1 In *Buffy* lore, when a person is transformed into a vampire, they lose their soul, a.k.a. their humanity. They hunt, kill, and maim, feeding on humans without the burden of a conscience. One hundred forty-five years into his life as a vampire, Angel's soul was restored (that is to say, he was re-ensouled) as a punishment, forcing him to experience a century and a half's worth of guilt and shame for his evil deeds all at once, and ultimately setting him on a lifelong quest for redemption.

together somewhat, sourcing bags of animal blood from the local butcher and spiking his hair (without even the aid of a mirror, as vampires cast no reflection). While he knows that he can never truly make up for all the pain and destruction he caused during his many years as a violent and murderous vampire, he is determined to never stop trying. An upsettingly hot, damaged man tortured by his dark past? He is what we call "the total package."

After months of fighting side by side with Angel against every manner of evil Sunnydale can offer, Buffy decides she is ready to share the deepest of intimacies with her first true love. Alas, in the moments just after, while they are naked and tangled in his red satin sheets, it is revealed that a single moment of true happiness is the exact trigger that *reverses* the curse that has maintained Angel's humanity for the past hundred years. As Buffy sleeps beside him, Angel is awakened to the terrifying realization that his soul is being ripped from his body. The soulless vampire Angelus[2] has returned in the place of Angel, and he spends the following months hell-bent on destroying a devastated Buffy and all those she holds dear.

His campaign of terror includes but is not limited to stalking Buffy, sending her charcoal portraits he sketched of her while she was sleeping, and violently murdering Jenny Calendar. When these activities fail to satisfy Angelus's bloodlust, he decides that the next logical step is opening a portal to a hell dimension that will swallow Sunnydale and the rest of Earth along with it.

Buffy, already torn apart by the dark transformation of her beloved, learns that there is—as there always seems to be—a

---

2 Since Angel is *clearly* not a name for an evil vampire, "Angelus" is the name our broody boy goes by when he is sans soul.

catch: the portal can only be closed by the blood of whoever opened it.

And so, Buffy is forced to choose between killing the man she loves and allowing the world to end. Facing the Master was clear-cut: good versus evil, win or lose. But this time, any choice that she makes will result in profound loss.

In the time before
My life a thousand open doors
Light and full with possibility

Jenny

During our first Christmas back on the East Coast, we spent time with our families and enjoyed the comfort of annual traditions like the Russo Family Christmas Eve Volcano—an initiative spearheaded by Kristin's sister, Aly, straight out of elementary school science class; that year the theme was "whale"[3]— and the Russo Family Christmas Eve Argument About Where to Set Off the Volcano, a collaboration between Aly and Kristin's mother, Rose, who was deeply concerned about the health

---

3 I invested a great deal of time, tape, and cardboard constructing the underlying shape of the beast, upon which Aly added homemade playdough, dyed blue with food coloring, to create the skin. The volcano was, of course, positioned to erupt from the whale's blowhole.

and well-being of her carpets and furniture, and who did not have volcano insurance.

Also during that same trip, we decided to reach out to a close friend to ask what felt like an insane question: Would he be comfortable giving us some of his sperm so that we might try to have a baby?

This wasn't our first step on the road toward becoming parents. Before our move west, we'd picked out a donor from a vast catalog supplied by a sperm bank. Since we'd already established that Kristin was going to carry, I took on the parental responsibility of isolating our donor pool to only the Charlie Hunnam look-alikes so that our future baby would have increased odds of sharing some of my features (and would also maybe be inclined to join a cool motorcycle gang).[4] We purchased some Hunnam-adjacent vials, shipped them from the sperm bank in California to a specialized storage facility in New York, and then wound up shipping them *back* to California when we decided to make our move across the country.

For most of my adult life, I'd had no interest in starting a family. I hadn't spent much time around babies, and definitely did not experience the pull of what you might call maternal instinct. The closest thing to parenting that I could easily envision was cohabitating with some kind of regal, short-haired hound, possessed of a certain quiet wisdom, to be found more often than not curled up before a roaring fireplace while I sipped something smoky and high proof from a snifter. But as

---

4 If you've never perused a sperm bank catalog, one thing the bank does—to give prospective sperm buyers a mental picture of the person whose genetic material they might be inviting into their family—is to include "celebrity look-alikes" with every donor listing. We'll take three Clooneys and a Pitt, please!

more and more of my friends became parents, the expanding love in their lives fanned a little ember in my heart, and suddenly the idea of adding a child to our family of two seemed a great deal more exciting.

Of course, if anyone had bothered to tell me about the downright science-fictioniness of trying to create a pregnancy outside of the, er, "traditional" method, I probably would have gotten on board much sooner. At the start of our process, Kristin and I would drive from one end of LA County to the other to pick up a canister that looked like it came straight out of *Jurassic Park,* complete with dry-ice vapor that would come spilling out when the vacuum-sealed lid popped open. Then we'd defrost small vials of frozen sperm while wearing winter gloves, and use a sterile plastic syringe from CVS to pop the frozen Hunnams into Kristin's body. When this method (unsurprisingly) did *not* result in pregnancy, we tried three more times with the help of local midwives. By December we were all out of our frozen sperm supply and disappointingly still not pregnant.

With our bank account dwindling (sperm is expensive, actually!) and our morale flagging, we determined that a change of course was in order. And so from the threshold of winter, we carefully composed "The Weirdest Most Bizarre E-Mail (We Have Ever Written)"—that was the actual subject line—and sent it to our friend in the hope that he might share with us just a little bit of his genetic material. Did we make jokes about the television series *Buffy the Vampire Slayer* in the body of this email? Yes indeed. Did we quote Whitney Houston to assure our donor that, regardless of the ultimate outcome, we would always love him? You bet. Did the phrase "whose sperm we covet" appear? It sure did.

Hitting Send on the email felt like when you tell someone you have a crush on them and then wait in agony to see if their feelings are returned. Lucky for us, we sent the email at 8:43 A.M. (in retrospect, perhaps an early hour for such a request), and we received a reply at 9:48 A.M. Sixty-five minutes! Surely a world record for an exchange of information concerning sperm. Our potential donor wasn't rushing to say *Yes, of course take my sperm*; he simply wanted to tell us how honored he was to have been asked, and that he knew it must have been a really vulnerable request to send, so he wanted us to know he had received it. What a guy, honestly. He told us he would be talking to his partner and that they'd respond more thoroughly soon. A few days later they told us that this was something they were eager to learn more about, and we made a plan to have dinner when we returned to Los Angeles in early January.

We flew back west on January 4, almost exactly one year to the day after our cross-country move. In addition to readying for our Very Special Sperm Donor Dinner, we also had a podcast recording schedule to resume. In the Season 2 premiere of *Buffy*, "When She Was Bad," our Slayer struggles with the posttraumatic stress of *literally dying*. Sure, in the end Buffy triumphed over the Master, but visions of being drowned continue to haunt her, distracting her from looking forward—or even being present—as her junior year of high school begins. By the end of the episode, Buffy has gotten her hands on the bones of the Master and chooses a path of catharsis not available to most: she smashes the skeleton of her enemy to dust with a sledgehammer.

While we didn't have a sledgehammer or the bones of our most recent enemy on hand—the former a bit easier to come by but the latter surely not impossible—considering the possibility of creating new life felt like a balm on the wounds of the previous year.

The night of our Very Special Sperm Donor Dinner arrived. When the doorbell rang, though every fiber of our beings told us to hide under the couch and pretend we had never existed, we convinced ourselves to answer the door. The four of us stood together in the living room for far too long and made far too many bad jokes, eventually moving our various sets of reproductive organs to the dinner table. We talked about our feelings. We talked about the legal implications. We talked about music, television, and the weather. We talked about everything we could think of until there was nothing left to talk about but the prospect of collecting specimen cups of sperm mere feet from where we currently sat. (As we'd learn in the months that would follow, what can seem impossibly awkward and endlessly bizarre will, with repetition, become just as normal an activity as brushing your teeth.) Before dinner ended that night, our friends said yes, they would be happy to help us on our way toward parenthood!

We celebrated our newfound sperm supply with ice cream at our favorite spot in Highland Park, and after about a month of getting the right legal paperwork in place, we embarked on a very strange and exciting quest.

The comedy of it all was very real. Our first misstep was setting out a hilariously large mason jar in the guest room on our donor's first visit (next to a vintage *Playboy*, just for fun). He looked at us, amused. "So you both have no idea about the quantity of this situation, do you?" (We did not.) We moved to more appropriately sized (and, for god's sake, *sterile*) specimen cups the following month.

The first several tries did not result in pregnancy, but did grease the wheels of the machine. By the third month we had a system in place: Our donor would arrive, we'd hang out for a bit, then he'd retreat to the guest room while we waited outside in our car, trying to give the man as much privacy as possible. When he completed the assignment, he would notify us by sending some kind of on-theme GIF to our group text thread (think ocean waves crashing foamily into rocks, rocket ships blasting off into the stratosphere, Katy Perry shooting whipped cream out of her bra in the "California Gurls" music video, etc.). That was our cue to go back inside, where Kristin would temporarily store the specimen cup in her bra (WARMTH!) while we said our good-byes, and then we'd go to *our* room and complete the process.

As we carefully navigated the ferrying of cups of sperm back and forth in our home, Season 2 of *Buffering* continued onward. We were also planning our first live recording of the podcast at the iconic NerdMelt Showroom, a comedy and pod-cast venue tucked in the back of the Los Angeles comic book shop Meltdown.[5]

On the night of the event, the room was full, and we were delighted to see some folks wearing T-shirts emblazoned with the *Buffering* logo. To get the party started, Kristin had lovingly crafted a modified version of the *Buffy* Season 2 credits, inte-grating both of us into the mix; when the first few organ notes of the *Buffy* theme song played at the start of the video, the crowd went wild. When a photo of me wielding a large scythe and grinning maniacally (just another Tuesday!) appeared on-screen, they *lost* it, and they saved just as much lung power for the reveal of Kristin's photo, where she is sipping demurely from a mug labeled MALE TEARS. When the video ended, we walked onstage. More screaming?! We were stunned, we were thrilled, we were *so excited*. A room full of enthusiastic Scoo-bies, all there to have a blast while we talked about *Buffy*?! What more could we ask for?

We had gathered together to discuss the fifth episode of the

---

5 The closing of this very cool spot in 2018 was a heartbreaking loss to lovers of comics, comedy, and podcasts in Los Angeles and beyond.

season, "Reptile Boy," in which evil frat boys chain up Buffy and Cordelia in their basement, attempting to pay tribute to the giant demon snake that supplies them with power and success in exchange for the occasional sacrifice of a young woman. The event would go down in *Buffering* history as the time that I spoiled a major character's death live onstage,[6] and also as the inspiration for our bestselling shirt of all time: two lizards wearing frat-appropriate hats (one fedora, one trucker), encircled by the phrase SMASH THE DEMON LIZARD PATRIARCHY.

That May, knee-deep in subterranean reptile demons and outsourced sperm, we found out we were pregnant.

Somehow, in spite of all the deliberate effort that led up to this moment, the arrival of a positive pregnancy test managed to take us by complete surprise. Kristin had become so accustomed to the disappointment of getting her period that when she was a few days late, she took the pregnancy test with divided attention, just before heading out for an appointment.

She waited alone in the bathroom for the plastic stick to tell her what she already knew: we weren't pregnant, again. Instead, when the stick flashed PREGNANT,[7] she came staggering across the hallway into the studio, where I was noodling on the song for "Phases" (the fifteenth episode of the season, in which Willow first learns that her boyfriend, Oz, is also a werewolf). Hand shaking, Kristin held up the stick; my vision went in and out of focus and my brain became the kind of spinning rainbow ball that indicates your computer is "working on it" (and might be about to crash). We froze, eyes locked together

---

6 *Buffering the Vampire Slayer* formally apologizes to anyone who entered NerdMelt that night unaware of the impending demise of Jenny Calendar.

7 Okay, look, I know that in reality the stick showed a smiley face or a pink plus sign rather than shouting the word "pregnant," but that's what it *felt* like.

in that tiny room in our rented Altadena home, and laughed and laughed and laughed.

We got blood work done right away—first to confirm the pregnancy, then a few more times to make sure things were moving along properly. Kristin installed an app on her phone that guesstimated—in exclusively fruit and vegetable comparisons—the size of our would-be child. We began with a sweet pea.

"Did you know the baby is *sprouting eyes* right now???" Kristin squealed to me in week five, and I delighted in the incomprehensibility of the information.

In week six, we proudly graduated to a blueberry. (A blueberry *with eyes*?!) Most of our conversations in the house during those first few weeks existed inside a space of imagining. We'd turn the guest room into the nursery. We had a backyard where we could suddenly envision the baby rolling around in the grass.

Even though it was early, we couldn't help ourselves and excitedly told Kristin's sister the good news. Aly was so thrilled that she couldn't help *herself* and took us out to dinner, gifting us a gorgeous set of baby blankets—which then prompted our waiter to congratulate Kristin and me on becoming parents. We, of course, told our donor and his partner. They were overjoyed, and days later we came home to a bouquet of flowers in a glass vase at our front door. The card attached wished us our very first Happy Mother's Day.

Kristin

When I was a kid, there were babies and pregnant women *everywhere*.

With seven aunts on my mom's side alone, our extended family had at least one new baby every year for twenty-five years. This meant that at all of our (many, many) family gatherings, aunts and uncles would make food and drink wine and beer while those of us kids who were old enough to walk around made sure that those who were still crawling or not yet mobile stayed alive.

One of my uncles took endless hours of home videos during these years on his ten-pound camcorder. Sometime in high school, I remember watching footage from a Fourth of July barbecue in which I, at age eight, walked through the camcorder's shot with my one-year-old cousin Michael tucked under one of my arms like a little pink football. By the time I was ten I would often pretend I was pregnant, holding my lower back as I sat down and imagining what it would be like when I could be just like my aunts (whom I idolized), waddling around with a big belly, laughing as my other four kids played with each other in the backyard.

Over the years, of course, my understanding of both pregnancy and parenting shifted—as did my romanticized visions of having multiple children smooshed into station wagons and small, two-bedroom homes. While I remain endlessly in awe of my aunts—who seemed to survive their earliest years of parenting with energy sourced solely from red wine, cigarettes, and rosary beads—by the time I was in my twenties I was focused on the idea of having a more manageable brood. I figured I would have two children by the time I was in my early thirties.

My early thirties came a lot sooner than I'd imagined (as they tend to do), and since Jenny and I only began dating when I was twenty-nine, I set a more specific goalpost for myself: Jenny and I would get married by the time I was thirty-two and then I would have our first child. This would give me a couple of years to still have our second child before I was thirty-five. Doing this kind of math, as I would learn in increasingly cruel ways over the years that followed, completely disregarded the very complicated and unpredictable process of trying to have a baby. During my first year of trying to get pregnant, a midwife spoke the truth to me more clearly than anyone ever had (and probably ever will). She said, "Getting pregnant is 100 percent science and 100 percent magic."

I monitored my body in what felt like a million ways, taking my temperature when I woke up every day, peeing on little paper sticks that could help us better predict when I might be ovulating. Each time we'd do an insemination, every sensation in my body felt like a sign of some kind. A cramp could mean the embryo had implanted! My boobs being sore could mean it had really happened this time! But cramps and soreness, each time, actually just meant that my period was near. We went through all the frozen sperm and still I was not pregnant. It wasn't until our fourth try with a new donor that we finally achieved the 100 percent science and 100 percent magic that we needed. After decades of imagining it and years of shaping the wish to fit my own life and my own partnership, it was here. I was pregnant.

Three weeks after we learned that I was pregnant, our work took us to the Midwest. In addition to making the podcast, we also both worked at an adult sleepaway camp for queer and trans folks at the time; I ran the camp as a codirector, and Jenny had been invited to come for several years as a musical performer. This year, for the first time ever, the camp was being hosted in Wisconsin instead of its usual site in California.

Camp was a very magical place, lovingly curated by a gaggle of queers that included bird watchers, strippers, jewelry makers, gender studies majors, medical doctors, sex experts, athletes, musicians, and more. Hundreds of queer folks would fly in from across the country (some even from across the world) to immerse themselves in five full days of offerings as varied (and as gay) as could be imagined. You could start your morning by attending the Dana Fairbanks Memorial Tennis Playoffs, take a crash course in *shibari* rope bondage after lunch, drop in on Bitches Brew for a comprehensive history of women in beer making before dinner, and end the evening by roasting s'mores or dancing with your crush at the "unofficial" after-hours hot spot, Club Deer.

This particular year's programming also included a live recording of *Buffering the Vampire Slayer*. At 3 P.M. on Saturday, May 20, we were scheduled to gather with the campers inside the camp's auditorium space to record our coverage of the eighteenth episode of *Buffy*'s second season, "Killed by Death." We were always beholden to our recording schedule when it came to timing live events, so although there was nothing inherently queer about this episode's demon, a top-hatted beast with an underbite who fed on the lives of sick children, we figured we'd still have a good time.

On the first day of setting up camp, in the middle of the monumental but also hilarious task of sorting all of our workshop supplies (including but not limited to a bin for nylon rope, a box for polymer clay, a bag for vibrators, and a tidy stack of paint sets), I noticed that I was spotting.

Spotting is totally normal, I told myself. (It is.)

The baby is fine, I told myself. (It was not.)

When Jenny and I first arrived in Wisconsin, she'd bought mountains of groceries at Whole Foods, stocking up so that the blueberry would receive its nutrients from organic grain bowls instead of the camp taco bar. She patiently spent every free moment of those first three days ensuring that I was hydrated, that I had food anytime I was hungry (and even times when I was not), and bringing me anything else my body needed while

I set up the camp and readied for the arrival of four hundred very excited campers. In all of our many years together, Jenny was always happiest when she had a clear and defined way to take care of me, to show me—a person who thrived on *not* asking for help—that she wanted to help me, that she was *able* to help me, and, most critically, that she loved me. I think one of the best parts of the few weeks we had together as expectant parents is that they softened me to be able to accept more of Jenny's help—and, by extension, more of her love.

This being camp, we were bunked up with six other staff members. They were the only six people we had told about the pregnancy, as we assumed the tight quarters (paired with my sudden disinterest in whiskey) would make it close to impossible to keep a secret. I was still spotting the next day, but Jenny and I both held tight to the fact that this was *normal,* and since I know myself to be someone who often thinks that the sky might be falling, I pushed down the ever-growing feeling that something was wrong.

The morning after the campers arrived, my spotting shifted. I was now seeing red. Something was, actually, very wrong.

Since this was a space that centered the experiences of queer women, it only made sense that I found myself surrounded by an Avengers-like team of Miscarriage Preparedness. Out of the six people in our room, one of them had experience handling trauma and crises, and another had lost several pregnancies herself. Right next door to us was a camp staff member who just so happened to be a licensed OB/GYN. Out of the mere handful of people who had been let into our experience, it seemed each one had a specialized skill set; each of those became a different support to hold both Jenny and me up as things progressed.

That afternoon, my OB/GYN Avenger sat down with me

privately, asking me detailed questions about how I was feeling and what I was seeing. She explained that she didn't have the proper tools to make sure I was okay—it could be something that passed on its own, but there could be a blockage, and it was better to be safe. She calmly but firmly told me to look up nearby hospitals and make a plan for whenever I decided it was time to go to the ER. She calmly but firmly reminded me that she was there for anything I needed.

Jenny and I sat together on our camp bed, in a small room far away from our home, our two suitcases lying open on the brown-carpeted floor, and tried to make a plan. No matter how deep the hurt goes, the logistics always demand attending to. That evening there was going to be a concert, and so—since I wasn't in pain and since the bleeding had not gotten worse—we decided we would wait to go to the hospital until the next morning.

I vividly remember walking down the stairs to the theater, smiling at the hundreds of sweet camper faces I passed, and thinking, "I am having a miscarriage right now." They were blissfully unaware of everything swirling inside me. The dissonance was staggering.

Down in the theater, Jenny and I sat side by side. The lights dimmed. The show began.

The cramps got worse.

I started feeling dizzy.

"We have to go now," I whispered. Jenny—a classic hesitator—didn't hesitate.

It's possible that Jenny and I were never closer than we were that night. We moved as one; we barely had to exchange words to communicate.

She grabbed the van keys and we stood up and walked out. Those who knew, knew.

At about 12:30 A.M., we started the ninety-minute drive to Madison, where I'd read there was a hospital ranked nineteenth in the whole country. That felt worth the extra half hour, and offered some kind of strange reassurance at a moment when everything felt wildly out of my control, when something I'd wanted so badly was escaping my body.

One of my Avengers—the woman who'd lost several pregnancies of her own—texted me as Jenny pulled the van out of the parking lot, "I just wanted to let you know that I have been in this situation myself, as have so many. And we are, all of us, riding with you."

The pain I felt during our drive was the kind of pain where you can't sit still. I hovered above my seat for a good portion of our journey. For other parts, I pushed my body back into the seat cushion. I played the radio. I'm certain there's no way I could have heard Mariah Carey's "All I Want for Christmas" because it was May, but I have a memory of it anyway.

When we got to the ER, Jenny dropped me at the entrance before parking. It felt like I'd already bled more in those two hours than I'd ever bled in my entire life. I ran to the bathroom before checking in. There was more blood, and one massive clot, the vision of which will be burned into my mind forever.

Before I could think too much more about what was happening, I changed my pad (all that work, all that trying, and now there was nothing to do but just throw it away?) and met Jenny in the waiting room. We checked in.

"What brings you here today?"

"I am having a miscarriage," I said. "This is my wife and we are having a miscarriage."

We were suffering a loss so many miles from where either of us had ever called home, and we were also so afraid of how we might be spoken to or judged. To our relief, every doctor, nurse,

EMT, and receptionist seemed to cradle both of us, equally, in their care. They were treating us, a queer couple, as two parents suffering a loss. They were incredibly gentle, looking us in the eyes, apologizing for our loss, and explaining every single step of the process.[8]

They started with blood work and an ultrasound. The woman who administered the ultrasound told us both that she'd lost a pregnancy just two weeks before. Her husband had been traveling for work at the time. We shared a moment together; she understood.

"It seems to have been a complete loss," the doctor who saw us next said. He explained that although "complete loss" can be hard to hear, it was actually good. It meant that my body wasn't having trouble releasing the thing it needed to release. He was gentle and kind; he cared.

Shortly before we were discharged, a nurse with short-cropped hair approached us. She said, "I know about the camp where you work. Thank you for what you do. I'm so sorry for your loss."

What she meant was, "I am queer like you. I see you. I am so sorry for your pain."

The doctor gave us paperwork, a pamphlet about what to expect in the coming days, and a poem about losing a child that it took us two weeks to work up the courage to read. He told me that I could continue working at camp if I wanted, but that I had to be sure to get more blood work done when we got back to Los Angeles. It was 6 A.M. when we were finally discharged.

We were still moving as one person. We looked at each other a lot but didn't talk much. We didn't have to.

---

8 A lifetime's worth of thanks to the staff at the UW Health University Hospital.

We drove from the ER to the Holiday Inn in Madison, where we slept for four hours. When we woke up, we cried together, briefly, holding each other under the crisp, starched sheets. We joked about how much more comfortable our hotel bed was than our bed back at camp. We drove back in the van quietly. Holding hands.

Both of Us

When we pulled the van back into the campsite it was about noon, so we only had a few hours before we needed to be on-stage. We showered, we dressed, we hugged the friends who'd sent us off in the van the night before. Jenny called our donor, a lift Kristin could not bear. Apart from our small handful of Avengers, no one else at the camp knew Kristin had been pregnant, and no one else at the camp knew what we'd just moved through.

We walked over to the auditorium.

This wasn't the first time we'd pushed aside feelings of devastation in order to forge forward with our work inside the *Buffering* community, and it certainly wouldn't be the last. There was also, as we'd seen before and would see again, an immense amount of strength, joy, and power to be found within that community amidst our own losses. This particular audience was full of *Buffy*-loving queers who were hopped up on days of community events and hammock make-out sessions. The energy in the room was an immediate balm on our souls.

Our friends joined us in conversation onstage, and we laughed until we cried as Jenny described the monster of the week (He's got a top hat! He's got Spirit Halloween hair! He's got impossibly long digits!), beginning what would become a long (winded) tradition of adding the prefix "be-" to all words that struck her fancy when she referred to Der Kindestod as "be-hatted," "be-wigged," and "be-long-fingered."

Admittedly, despite the comedy, Der Kindestod is a particularly insidious demon. Late at night, he slinks into the pediatric wing at the Sunnydale Hospital to feed on the life force of ailing children, via a pair of dreadful suckers that nauseatingly extend out from his eye sockets on stalks. Always able to find the comedy amidst the horror, Jenny sang the episode's song to a delighted audience:

> *There's a demon that's ephemeral*
> *Down at Sunnydale General*
> *In the east side children's wing*
>
> *He's a creepy motherfucker*
> *Whose eyes are made of suckers*
> *And he's hungry for children*

For a couple of hours, at least, we forgot about everything that had just happened outside that room.

But when the taping was over, we slid back to the reality that was, for now, mostly our secret. Kristin still had a hospital bracelet around her wrist. Later we discovered Der Kindestod roughly translates to "child death."

Camp ended, and we returned to an empty house. The guest room, where we'd stood together imagining what color to paint the walls and where we'd put a crib, would remain just a guest room. The backyard, where we'd pictured a small child rolling around, crawling, maybe even toddling about, would stay just a backyard.

+ .+ .*.

In Sunnydale, Buffy ultimately makes the choice to sacrifice Angel, whom she loves dearly, to save the world. She knows that no matter how much she loves him, Angel's blood is the only thing that can close the portal to hell. She kisses him, tells him to close his eyes, and then plunges a sword through his chest.

While the seasons before and after this one end in a triumph that can be celebrated, Season 2 stands apart as one where, despite the world continuing to spin, it does so beneath a sky full of dark clouds.

BECOMING

In the time before, my life a thousand open doors
Light and full with possibility
Then came the call, a pull that I could not ignore
A bell that tolled for me and only me

Made me the loneliest girl in California

I turned to stone, life and death to focus on
Till a shadow left the wall and reached for me
The slightest smile, you walked beside me for a while
But mistakes we can't unmake ripped you away

From the loneliest girl in California

Deepest well, examination of myself
Reveals the way I know it has to be
Now comes the call, oh how I wish I could ignore
The bell that tolls for me and only me

And I'm the loneliest girl in California

A Scooby Brings Us Hellmath

In January 1998, at the midpoint of the television show's second season, Buffy and Angel consummated their relationship, and those of us watching in real time died screaming. We'd been waiting nearly a year for this moment. Finally, after they had kissed in the slatted light of many a mini blind, *it was happening*. Sometime between midnight and 4 A.M. Pacific Standard Time, under the light of a full moon, two souls came together . . . and then one was promptly evicted from its skeletal abode. After a brief postcoital nap, Angel shot upright and ran out the door, gasping and suddenly soulless in a rainstorm! *He was an evil vampire again!*

In April 2017, we died screaming all over again discussing these events on the podcast. As we examined the details of the plot, we were left wondering: Was there a formula to this dissolution? Was Angel's "one moment of true happiness" falling in love? Was it simply having an orgasm? Thankfully, beloved friend of the podcast Joanna Robinson had stopped by to help us reason it through. We all agreed that Angel must have fallen in love before Buffy, and certainly he'd had an orgasm sometime in the last century. This led us to conclude that it must be some combination therein.

Joanna, a lightbulb going off above her head, reasoned:

$$\heartsuit\text{TRUE LOVE}\heartsuit + \text{orgasm} = -1 \text{ soul}$$

We gasped. This was the first time that we'd had to deploy a mathematical equation to better understand what was happening in the town of Sunnydale, also known as the Hellmouth. We declared that any math done to serve a population within a fifteen-mile radius of the Hell*mouth* would henceforth be known as Hell*math*.

Once we started, we could not stop.[1]

Our second Hellmath symposium involved Angelus's eyeliner. In addition to his new homicidal mandate, the loss of Angel's soul seemed to inspire a number of related changes to our broody vampire: (1) as noted, he resumed going by his old (evil) name, Angelus; (2) his wardrobe became populated almost exclusively by half-buttoned shirts in velvets and silks; and (3) he developed a serious dependence on eyeliner. Was Angelus more glam than Angel, we wondered? The plot thickened, and by the plot, we mean the makeup. It seemed the longer his soul was absent, the more Sephora-given definition appeared around his eyes. Hellmath helped us see exactly how intensely the phenomenon progressed:

---

1 Nor could our listeners, as evidenced in Appendix A.

ANGELUS EYELINER WATCH

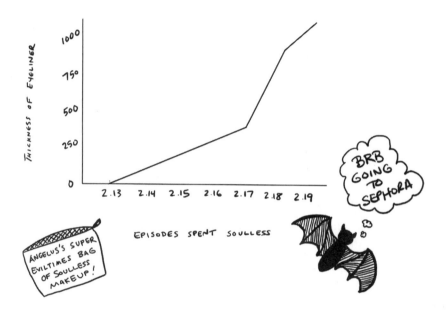

Exhibit A: Jenny's hard data on the relationship between Angelus, his eyeliner, and his time spent without a soul.

chapter three

WILD HORSES COULDN'T DRAG US AWAY

Buffy enters her senior year of high school with a more finely honed sense of self, forged at great cost in the fiery crucible of the preceding year. Mourning the loss of her brooding beau, and wracked with guilt over her hand in his banishment to a distant hell dimension, Buffy holds her grief alone at first. She is also carrying the weight of a heavy secret: she has told no one that Angel's soul was restored only seconds before she killed him. It is obvious to Giles that something is deeply wrong in Slayerville, and Buffy at last comes clean about what she had to sacrifice in order to save the world. It is this admission, saying it out loud to someone, that finally allows her to accept the truth of the matter: her true love is gone.

Except, of course, not quite.

Riding high upon the wave of her newfound acceptance, Buffy visits the last place she saw Angel alive—an old, abandoned house that we affectionately refer to as Vamp Mansion—with her fist clenched around the claddagh ring he gave her before their love took a turn for the tragic. She shares a quiet moment with the empty room and the memory of her lover, then kneels and places the ring in the middle of the floor as a final farewell. She turns around and leaves the way she came in. Fade to black.

Then . . . a bright light cuts through the murk to illuminate the ring, a deep rumbling sweeps through the room, and Angel falls naked (and for some reason very wet) from above, crashing gracelessly to the floor where the claddagh ring had been placed moments before.

Miraculously reunited, Buffy and Angel attempt to regain the relationship they once had. But as they spend more time together, Angel grows increasingly aware of all the things he knows he cannot offer her as a partner. As she gets older, he will remain the same age. If she ever wants to start a family, he won't be able to give that to her. They can't even share meals together. As the months pass, Angel realizes he cannot hold on to this love for love's sake alone, and that truly loving Buffy would mean leaving her so that she could find someone with whom she could grow.

Just days before they are set to go to the Sunnydale senior prom together, Buffy confronts Angel on his increasingly distant behavior. Angel finally comes clean and tells Buffy that he cannot stay with her, and will be leaving town after they finish their battle at graduation.

Buffy is, understandably, destroyed.

How could you and me ever be enemies
I thought you and me could never be enemies

Kristin

When the summer of 2017 did not bring us a child in human form, Jenny—reaching for something, *any*thing to fill the empty space in our home (and hearts)—pitched me on an interim concept: What about a cat? It had been almost two years since we'd said goodbye to our beloved Trey, and yet we still panicked when dresser drawers were left ajar, forgetting that he was no longer there to nestle himself between our shirts and socks. I had barely uttered the first syllable of the word "maybe" in response to Jenny's suggestion before she'd whipped out her phone and pointed to a photo of a kitten named Sam who was available for adoption. "What about *this* one, look look look, she is so very cute and sweet and has big saucer eyeballs and will probably be perfectly behaved and never make any mischief," she implored.

And so it was that a miniscule white-and-tan kitten who loved to chase after paper balls and unspool any roll of toilet paper that she could get her paws on came into our lives.

Sam, whom we also referred to as "Mini" (soon shortened to "Min"), "the Spring Peeper," "Welcome Back Trotter," "Samantha Mulder," and "Das Floof," was a four-month-old rescue who brought much-needed distraction and joy to what had been a very hard few months.

As soon as we walked in the door from the adoption clinic, I ran to the back of the house to get Sam settled. In the dining room, moments later, I heard a massive crash.[1] I sprinted back

---

1 This crash was decidedly louder than the ones I had become familiar with, such as the time earlier that year when, after the sound of breaking glass filled the house, I had called out to Jenny, "Are you okay?" and she responded, "I dropped some bowls." When I countered, "How many broke?" she replied swiftly, "All of them."

into the room to investigate and found Jenny standing in about an inch of water. With her attention focused on kittens and nothing more, she had absent-mindedly placed two five-gallon water jugs on the edge of our dining-room table. The sudden addition of weight instantly snapped one wooden leg of the table clean through, sending both jugs to the floor and spilling all ten gallons of water across our dining room (which we then efficiently swept out the door with a broom). It seemed that the excitement we had for this new, tiny life was big enough to break furniture and incite small floods.

As Sam busily climbed every piece of furniture in our home, we resumed monthly sperm parties with our donor. It's like the old saying goes: if at first you don't succeed, inseminate, inseminate again. *Buffering* was steadily growing in listeners, and that summer also saw the podcast reach a previously unimaginable milestone: we hit *one million* downloads. To mark the occasion, we took family photos with Sam, who wore a tiny party hat we'd handcrafted for her, adorned with a glittery number one.

This was also the same summer that we'd been invited to attend NYC's Flame Con, the world's largest queer comic convention. Imagine our surprise when, two weeks before we boarded a plane to New York for the convention, Jenny came home to an entirely unexpected and unprompted eviction notice taped to our front door. I was in the parking lot of the nearby BevMo!, having just stocked up on wine (my ritual at this point in our fertility journey was countering the gut punch of a negative pregnancy test with my own personal reward of wine and a cigarette), when I answered a phone call from a very frantic Jenny. Our exchange went something like this:

Jenny: WE ARE EVICTED.
Me: WHAT?

Jenny: WE. GOT. EVICTED.
Me: WHAT ARE YOU TALKING ABOUT?
Jenny: THERE IS AN EVICTION NOTICE ON OUR
   DOOR.
Me: WHAT?????[2]

Having a RAV4 full of wine had never been more timely.

In the span of fourteen days, we somehow managed to arrange a last-minute moving sale, pack everything we owned into boxes and bags, survive approximately twelve emotional meltdowns (mostly mine), locate a new place to live (which hilariously was two blocks away, on the same street as our current home), dump all of our boxes and bags into our new home, drop Sam off at a local cat hotel (an incredible wonderland where dozens of cats roam free), and board our flight at LAX.

I also happened to be ovulating, because *why not*? So amidst the chaos-on-chaos, we decided to fly our sperm donor across the country so that in between meeting and greeting, selling *Buffering* shirts, and taping our first live episode of the season, we could scoot upstairs to our hotel room and do a quick insemination.

We were physically, mentally, and emotionally exhausted, but we deliberately stored those feelings on a shelf waaaay at the tippy-top of our emotional pantry. Just how deep our exhaustion reached, and how it (and our choice to push it out of our minds) would affect us in the weeks and months to come, neither of us realized just yet.

We had a packed room once again for our live recording, this

---

2 We had never been late on rent and were meticulous in caring for the house and property. We reached out to our landlord, who had up to this point always been extremely warm and friendly, and received only a curt text telling us to direct any further communication to his lawyer. To this day, we have no idea why we were evicted!

time inside the Brooklyn Bridge Marriott Hotel. The episode of focus was the second of Season 3, "Dead Man's Party," in which Buffy's mom, Joyce, hangs up a new piece acquired by the gallery where she works: a mask . . . that raises the dead (classic).

Speaking of moms, both of my parents were also in the audience, getting their very first experience of our show. Jenny and I had been so excited about their attendance that we watched the episode *with* them before the taping, and so in our conversation onstage we included a running list of each time my mom had audibly gasped—including but not limited to when we first see the mask, when a zombie attacks Giles's car, when a college student dies at Sunnydale University, and when Joyce's friend Pat is killed (annotated by my mom with an, "Oh shit, she's one of *them* now!" after Pat then turns into a zombie).

The audience was incredible. They cheered for my parents, they laughed hysterically as Jenny sang a song about a zombie cat (oddly, also stored on a tippy-top shelf), and they converged en masse at our booth to shower us in love. It was a moving experience, to say the absolute least, made even more powerful by being in our home city of Brooklyn.

Two days before the premiere of our third season, a glowing profile on our partnership and our work together, titled "The Earth Is Not Doomed," was published on *Autostraddle*. The first paragraph read:

> *Jenny Owen Youngs is your best friend. Kristin Russo is your big sister. Or Jenny is the teen dream whose picture you'd have cut out of* Queer Tiger Beat *if it had been a thing when you were a youth. And Kristin is your mentor. Or Kristin would have been in* Queer Tiger Beat *and Jenny is the person whose voice you turned to driving around with the windows down sing-crying about being in unrequited love (with your best friend).*

The article was a heartwarming snapshot of the community that was forming around us, and a beautiful glimpse into how they spoke about us and our work (and our likelihood of being in *Tiger Beat*).

When we returned to Los Angeles, we picked up Das Floof from her cat hotel and headed to our new home.[3] Even though it was just a stone's throw away from our last home, its location on the opposite, uphill side of the street in the Altadena mountains meant that from our kitchen window we could now see all the way to downtown Los Angeles. There were terra-cotta-tiled floors, a skylight in the bathroom, and a fully finished basement where we were able to set up an even better home recording studio.

We began the task of unpacking the piles of bags and boxes we'd left behind before our trip to New York. While I had once worried that our good apartment fortune in Brooklyn might mean I would be karmically hit by a bus, I didn't experience the same anxiety in this new home. Since, in this instance, I was about to be hit by the biggest emotional bus of my lifetime and since these very same bags and boxes would be packed up again in less than one year's time . . . maybe, for once, I would have been right to worry.

Jenny

October 2017 marked the inaugural occurrence of what would become our annual tradition of dressing up in *Buffy* cosplay

---

3 Somehow Sam and I had both picked up horrendous colds during our trip to New York. Sam had clearly gotten hers from the cat hotel and, while there's a small chance that perhaps I got my own cold from the queer masses at Flame Con, I insisted to Jenny that I had contracted "kennel cough" from Sam.

for Halloween. We had recently covered a fan-favorite episode from the third season, "Band Candy," in which all of the adults in town revert to teenage versions of themselves (a side effect of consuming some cursed fundraising chocolate on sale to benefit the marching band). Many hijinks ensue, including Joyce Summers (a.k.a. Buffy's *mom*) and Giles having S-E-X on the hood of a cop car. Twice. In tribute, Kristin wound a feather boa around her neck and dangled a pair of handcuffs from one finger as Joyce, I rolled up a pack of cigarettes in the sleeve of my white T-shirt as Giles, and we even dressed up tiny Sam as a bar of chocolate.

In November, we celebrated Christmas in Sunnydale with our coverage of "Amends," in which the subterranean location of a great and powerful evil is given away by a ring of dead Christmas trees found inside the local tree lot (directly above said evil at ground level). Perhaps in an effort to keep our lives and the lives of Sunnydale residents feeling somewhat synchronized, perhaps as a portent of darknesses yet to come, or perhaps just because there was a horrible drought that year, our own Christmas tree perished prematurely, only a week after we brought it home. Since Kristin's family was coming to spend Christmas with us on the West Coast that year, we rushed to obtain a second tree to replace the withered one before their arrival.

We hosted Christmas Day at our new home. Kristin's mom, Rose, made a sage-colored runner for our dining-room table and we decorated it with tea lights and pine sprigs (of the unwithered variety). We got dressed up and sat together around a meal consisting of various plates made by each of us: we'd roasted a turkey, Rose had made a giant spread of roasted vegetables and mashed potatoes, and Kristin's sister had brought over stuffing and apple pie. The evening began beautifully, and a photo of us all around the table would suggest that the visit was picture-perfect as well.

But so much fell outside the frame. After the meal was finished, the wine continued to flow. When the plates were cleared, Rose broke down crying over the loss of her would-be grandchild. Kristin's dad, Pete, usually the most jovial in any group, was acting strangely distant; three years later, he would be diagnosed with dementia, and looking back, this seems to have been one of the earliest hints of what was to come. Kristin and I held ongoing arguments in whispers behind closed doors. It seemed like we couldn't stop fighting about small things—so small that today we cannot remember what any of them were.

Meanwhile, in podville, we announced an event different from anything else we'd done up to this point. *Buffy* Prom was an idea we'd come up with early on in Season 3, knowing that Buffy herself would be attending prom at the end of her senior year. We also knew that many of the people who loved *Buffy* dearly, and who were finding community through the podcast, may never have gone to a prom (including me!). Or, if they had attended, perhaps they had not been able to do so as their authentic selves, or alongside the person they'd wanted to bring. We thought it would be fun to have our own little punch fountain and a photo booth, get decked out in fancy clothes, and dance the night away to nineties jams.

We knew that our listeners would be excited, but we had no understanding of just *how* excited. Tickets sold out in less than three minutes! We had severely underestimated the power of what we were offering. A magical evening, we hoped. A convergence of *Buffy* folk making merry together, to be sure. But maybe most importantly, we were creating an opportunity—the rarity of which did not fully dawn on us until after prom night had come and gone: a "do-over" for a rite of passage that thrills and haunts the American imagination in equal measure. We hoped to revamp (pun intended) the concept of a night to remember, and make sure it was a night you *wanted* to remember.

In between announcing prom and actually *hosting* prom, I flew to New York for a couple of weeks, to work on an album with my longtime friend and collaborator Bess Rogers and her husband, Chris Kuffner. Bess and Chris had a home studio in Windsor Terrace where we'd be working. They also had a new son named Orion, and in the interest of trying not to impose on their new parenthood any more than our recording schedule already was, I made plans to stay with friends in another part of Brooklyn. The two locations were relatively close as the crow flies, but as I am not a crow, I was bound to the limitations of public transportation; my commute between studio and lodging required an hour of walking and training each morning and again each night. When I arrived back at the apartment in the evenings, my hosts were often out. I started to feel like a person who lived alone, and spent nearly all my waking hours working on music. The normal flow of my life in Los Angeles—meetings, writing sessions, multitasking, podcasting—was paused and put away. With my attention undivided by other creative pursuits, and only minimally pulled by social engagement with anyone outside of my collaborators, something began to happen that had not happened in a very long time: my mind became very quiet.

People are so incredibly adaptable; we can get used to almost anything. This is one of our greatest powers as a species, and an effective foil against the human brain's seemingly bottomless desire to maneuver us into all sorts of uncomfortable situations. Sometimes when I'm working at a computer for a while, I'll suddenly come back to my body and realize I'm leaning rather far forward in my chair—in an effort, I suppose, to get my nose pressed up against the screen—shoulders hunched, eyes squinting against the light of a screen that's a little too bright, especially in comparison to the room, which has darkened considerably since I was last aware of it, say an hour or two ago. When this awareness comes, my body doesn't feel *good*. My neck hurts, I feel stiff, I might have a headache. But my brain rerouted those signals while I was working, sent them to a holding tank, because it was consumed with the tasks at hand and did not want to be distracted. We are amazing at deprioritizing messages we do not want to receive.

But in New York, when my mind became less noisy, I started to notice something.

It was a sort of low hum, the kind of background noise we filter out automatically and ignore. But it got louder. And louder. As the volume increased, the hum gradually clarified itself from a hazy cloud to words I could almost read if I squinted; from there it grew clearer still until not only did I know the words, but I found myself unable to make them go away. My brain said:

something is wrong something is not right something is wrong something is not right something is wrong something is not right something is wrong something is not right

The hum was not truly unfamiliar to me. These words had been transmitting in the background for some time, longer than I cared to consider. But I had been carefully shushing them, stuffing them back into the darkest corners of my skull. I didn't *want* something to be wrong. I didn't want it to mean what most of me already knew it meant.

Kristin

Despite the trauma of our recent miscarriage and how much each negative pregnancy test hurt after that loss—or, in retrospect, perhaps as a result of that pain—we decided to up our odds of getting pregnant again by working directly with a fertility clinic. As we planned for our first *Buffy* Prom, our new doctor called to explain that there seemed to be an error in my initial blood work. One of the values seemed off to her, and so rather than start in February, she suggested we redo the panel and skip my next cycle, beginning inseminations in March instead.

At the time, the suggestion of taking even one month off from trying, and trying, and trying again felt at first like an impossibility. In many ways, the endless cycles of monitoring and attempting to make myself a hospitable living space for a child had left me feeling like my body was no longer my own. It had been an entire year of the same loop. Morning after morning, I would wake up and take my temperature and then stumble, still half-asleep, into our bathroom to pee on an ovulation predictor stick, charting all of my facts and figures in an app on my phone.[4] If I couldn't control the magic required to make a baby, I could at least double and triple down on the science of it all. I didn't travel as much as I once had, I was increasingly careful about what I ate (sweet potatoes can help with fertility, my doctor had once told me; spinach had folic acid), how I exercised (regular workouts were good, but nothing too strenuous after an insemination; if I swam laps in the pool, could the water be cold enough to negatively affect an embryo??), and my mental health (I should do more breathing exercises; had I miscarried because I worried too much?). While our move west had certainly made me feel isolated and far from home, the years of reaching (grasping, even) toward pregnancy had amplified those feelings a hundredfold.

---

4 Years later I still have mornings where my mind unconsciously flips back to this time and causes me to panic in the middle of peeing, my brain screaming, "DON'T FORGET THE STICK!"

So although the idea of pausing the pregnancy spin cycle felt all kinds of wrong, it also felt like maybe—just maybe—I could use a moment for myself. I had not been back east since our trip to Flame Con the previous summer, and Jenny happened to have recording sessions coming up in NYC. I decided to join her for the last week of her trip. I could get some much-needed time with my friends, I could eat some bagels, I could take a nice, deep breath before returning west to begin it all again.

Sometimes I wish I could go back to that February. I wish that *this* iteration of me, a future-me who is more calloused and world-weary, could go back to 2018 and find *that* iteration of me, the one who didn't know yet, the one who was softer and more vulnerable. I wish that somehow I could find her and tell her to put on even the smallest bit of armor; that I might warn her in some way about all that was about to unfold as she boarded that plane to New York.

Despite Jenny and me being in our home city for a full week together, we spent most of the trip apart. Jenny was working long days and long nights, so I planned dinners with friends on my own and spent the days visiting my favorite coffee spots, working in my favorite libraries, and trying to get some of myself back from inside the always-loud, perfectly chaotic, endlessly loving embrace of my New York. Even in the small moments when Jenny and I did see each other, she seemed to be somewhere far away. Something about our inter-actions made me feel like she was angry with me—like, even though we were doing our own separate things in a city we loved, I had pushed myself into a place where I was not wanted.

While I was not unfamiliar with Jenny feeling far away, and especially so when she was deep at work in a creative space, this felt different. I asked her on my second day in the city if she was okay. I asked her if *we* were okay. "Of course," she said. "Of course."

I chose to believe her.

+ .+ . + .

We were still in New York when Valentine's Day arrived, and I posted a photo of myself kissing a very sexy everything bagel, jokingly explaining that I was spending this Valentine's Day with my "one true love." A few hours later I saw that Jenny had also posted to Instagram—a series of photos of her and me together with the message, "Happy Valentine's Day to #1 wife, podcasting partner, and cat co-parent. The teen Joyce to my teen Giles, she's quite literally the very best person I've ever met, and she cracks me up like nobody else." It was more romantic and loving than nearly anything I had ever seen Jenny write publicly, and I felt equal parts touched and guilty (I had only posted about my mistress, the bagel!). I posted again, this time a black-and-white photo of Jenny onstage, scream-singing her heart out and clutching her guitar. "One more Valentine's Day confession," I wrote. "I love this person."

Two days before we went back to Los Angeles, Jenny joined me on an overnight trip upstate. My best friend, Randi, had just purchased a home two hours north of the city, and we were excited to get to see the new house in its "before" state; Randi and her wife were still living full time in Brooklyn at that point, and a few weeks later massive renovations were scheduled to begin. Before dinner, the four of us took a long walk down by the stream that ran through their backyard; the winter is the best time for a river walk in the woods of upstate

New York because the ground is frozen—there's no mud, there are no bugs, and things are at their most peaceful.

That night, curled up on an air mattress in one of the spare rooms, I could not fall asleep. After tossing and turning and finally succumbing to slumber, I dreamed of holding our baby. I put the baby carefully in its car seat and then watched in helpless horror as strangers came and took the baby away. They put the baby in their car and sped off as I remained frozen, unable to move. I woke up gasping for air. I explained the dream through sobs to Jenny, who held me, sang to me, and helped calm me. We both slept restlessly for what remained of the night and headed back in the morning for our last night together in Brooklyn.

That last night we spent at Randi's Brooklyn apartment, 644 Warren Street, lovingly referred to as just "644." It had first been home to Randi and her then-girlfriend Erin in 2010 after another lesbian couple moved out and tipped Erin off to the good location and unbeatable rent. When Erin and Randi broke up, Randi stayed at 644 solo for a year before Jenny and I both moved in with her and we lived as a trio for several months; when we eventually moved to our own place in Brooklyn, Randi stayed and went on to live there with her next partner, whom she would marry. After they moved upstate, they passed it on to our good friends, another queer couple. It was a space that had been in our lives for nearly a decade, and that night we were sleeping on a foldout mattress in the room that had once been ours.

Once again, I could not fall asleep. Something felt wrong in my bones. Even though Jenny was right next to me, she felt miles away. She'd seemed either completely absent or intensely romantic and caring in waves for the past week, and, like I was some kind of Goldilocks, nothing felt right. I asked her again. "Is something wrong?" This time, her response was different.

Jenny is someone who chooses her words very carefully. She thinks through the various ways she might phrase a statement or a feeling, sifts through them to make sure she is choosing the ones that most precisely match her meaning, and only then does she speak. In the beginning of our relationship, I would constantly interrupt these silences, begging her to speak her mind *while* she thought. Over the years, I learned that we processed differently, and that she needed that time, so I had grown accustomed to sitting and waiting for her to gather her words. Still, the silence between my question and her answer felt like a hundred million years. Through tears she said, "I feel wrong. Something feels wrong." Another long pause. "I don't feel like myself in our marriage."

The world fell out of its orbit.

The flight home the next morning was a living hell. We couldn't talk without crying, so we took turns writing things down in a notebook and passing it back and forth to each other, trying to express how we were feeling, trying to sort any way forward that didn't feel like it was aimed directly at an ending. "How can I help you feel more like yourself?" I wrote. "Should we open up our marriage?" "Do you still love me?" "I can stop trying to get pregnant while we work through this." "I love you." People seated around us were polite enough not to stare, but we definitely didn't make it easy.

All of this unfolded just two and a half weeks before we were set to host our very first (and very sold out) *Buffy* Prom in Los Angeles. Nothing seemed real. This simply could not be happening.

I spent the next two weeks divided between planning all the final details of our biggest event to date—which included frequent visits to the Ace Hotel to plot out the best location for the stage, sort how the sound system worked, discuss custom cocktails, and organize balloon rentals and cakes and ticket check-in processes—and grasping at ways to save my marriage. I obsessively read books by Esther Perel. I purchased us a set of three notebooks—one for me to write down my own feelings, one for Jenny to write down hers, and one for us to use to write to each other. I bought a new bra. Maybe if the solution wasn't found in sharing our feelings, a bit of lace could help.

Jenny, with my encouragement, spent long days away from the house in conversation with her close friends. At the time, I believed that they would help guide her back to me, back to us. Once she got the space she needed to take a deep breath, this would all be okay.

We did not break from our podcasting schedule. The week we returned from New York, we recorded our coverage of Season 3's "Choices," and the following weekend we broadcast from our living room for a live watch of "Doppelgangland" with our listeners. We were good at pretending that everything was okay. We were masters at compartmentalizing. When we got to the twentieth episode of the season, "The Prom," we invited the incredible Ira Madison III to be our special guest. He came to our home, knowing nothing of its broken center as we discussed Buffy's shattered heart and Angel's decision to leave their relationship (and Sunnydale) right after dancing one last dance with Buffy.

Days passed, and things only got worse. We slept apart most nights. Jenny slept downstairs in our basement studio space, where we had a guest bed set up. Sam didn't know what to do, where to sleep, or why we now spent hours screaming or sobbing at each other from the top and bottom steps of the stairway that divided our home.

When we were preparing to try to get pregnant, we had begun seeing a couples therapist. If we were going to add another human to this family dynamic, we'd reasoned, we owed it to ourselves and our future child to try to shake the Etch A Sketch on any existing conflict in our relationship. When we brought this news to our next session, our therapist told us that sometimes people in our position continue therapy to try to stay together, and others continue as a means to help them move apart. What were we there to do?

I wanted to work. I wanted to stay together.

Jenny said she did not know.

It was only a week later that Jenny came in from another day away, this time walking up the terra-cotta-tiled stairs that led to our front door with her notebook in hand. We'd just gotten a new couch, a bright-blue velvet three-seater that sat underneath a gorgeous print of Yellowstone Park. She sat on the arm of the couch. I sat at the opposite end, facing her. She read to me, and while there are many details that neither of us will ever revisit, the crux of her message was, "I am leaving. This is over."

Buffy Prom was six days away.

The world continued to plummet.

There was more crying, more yelling, more minutes and hours spent feeling horrible apart and horrible together. I spent those days insisting that this reality was *not* reality, unspooling mountains of reasons why we needed more time, more work, more anything that wouldn't mean this was happening. We had been together for almost ten years. We had been married for nearly five. How could all of that end inside the span of four weeks?

We struggled to complete the song for "The Prom." Jenny's task of writing from the perspective of Buffy, who, like me, was devastated and reaching for the one she loved, was too tall an order. The lyrics eventually became a simple refrain, repeated again and again: *If I can't stop you from leaving / what am I gonna do / what am I gonna do.*

The next time we went to therapy, Jenny had her answer—and her answer had to also define mine. We were here to move apart.

Many of the moments that followed are lost to a body's need to bury its worst hurts, but coming home from that therapy session remains my most vivid memory from that entire horrible year. When the door to our home opened, my eyes settled first on all of our books together on their shared shelves, alphabetical by author. There was nothing I could think of to say except the word "no." No, this cannot be happening. No, this is an impossibility.

My eyes scanned farther into our home and, without meaning to, I kept saying that same word countless times—over and over in a refrain. Looking at that new blue couch we'd just bought, the mantel where we'd only just taken down our three stockings (Sam's with a tiny *s* on the cuff), yesterday's pile of mail on the small secretary desk in the entryway, Sam's "burger and fries" catnip toys on the runner in the hallway, the jars in which we stored our coffee and our tea, our matching fucking slippers, our bed, our whole home, our whole life. No no no no no no no no no no.

Somewhere in the middle of all of those noes, Jenny got back in the car and drove away. I don't know where she went, but even then, I knew that it was no longer possible for us to be in the same physical space as we both fell to pieces.

Jenny

I came home from that trip to New York with what felt like an anvil in my stomach. I knew what I had to do, and yet it was absolutely unthinkable. My brain dutifully haunted me with a host of doubts: What if I was making a huge mistake? What if there was some obvious truth I was overlooking? What if I left my marriage and then found a Kristin-shaped hole in my life? I had been known to be my worst enemy when it came to relationships. I needed someone I trusted to hear me out, look me in the eye, and tell me if I was fucking up. I spent as much time as I could on the phone or in person with close friends, running down the facts, the feelings, and everything in between. I felt like I was toeing the edge of a massive drop, watching pebbles cascade down into the abyss, and I couldn't stop talking about it if I tried. I talked and talked and talked, thinking that maybe if I kept talking about it, I might never have to *do* something about it.

During this period, I darkened the doorstep of my close friend Molly, crashing at her apartment when I was at my lowest. "I think I'm . . . getting divorced," I said, slumping bonelessly down onto her couch.

I flipped numbly through her coffee-table books while she went into the kitchen to make us her house cocktail: mezcal, Topo Chico, and lime. She'd just been to Amoeba Music and picked up a vinyl copy of the latest St. Vincent album; she put it on, excited to listen top to bottom. But I immediately became fixated on the sidewinding melancholy of the first track, "Hang on Me," and made her repeatedly drop the needle at the beginning of the side every time the song ended.[5]

"The one thing I can say," she told me, measured and thoughtful as always, "is that I haven't seen your full self since you and Kristin got together." This hit like a mallet on a gong. I realized I felt the same way; where was the rest of me? Early on in our relationship I had been louder, wilder, and more chaotic. These

---

5 Sorry, Molly! But I will say I've had the song on loop while writing this section, and the repeat-listening approach *really* holds up for me.

elements had not seemed to fit in the context of my new partnership, and that had felt okay, more or less, because they were not necessarily qualities I wanted to maintain. But it was dawning on me now that perhaps in my efforts to tamp them down, I'd gone too far and misplaced other aspects of myself in the process. And while I had felt this on some unnamable level deep down inside me, knowing that my friends perceived it somehow felt much more disturbing than just having the feeling myself.

Molly left the room for a moment and came back holding a Polaroid camera. She told me, "Try to look exactly how you feel. A year from now, we'll look at this picture, and things will be better. You'll be able to laugh at it." In the photograph, I'm lying on my side on the couch, my head propped up in my right hand. My left hand is flashing a peace sign. My eyebrows are angled up, furrowing my forehead, and my eyes are lost in a thousand-yard stare. The picture does make me smile now. But it took a lot longer than a year.

+ ⊹ ·⊹·

The day of *Buffy* Prom arrived, and from a strictly practical perspective, it didn't matter that things between Kristin and me were nearly unbearable; the prom gods demanded we complete certain tasks in order to make possible a glorious and unforgettable evening for all Scoobies in attendance.

We drove from Altadena to downtown Los Angeles to drop off a carload of supplies at the Ace. Back inside the car, Kristin yelled while I stared out the window. We continued west to Party City, where we'd reserved three dozen maroon and gold helium-filled balloons. Under other circumstances, the clown show of us trying to cram all of them into one car, weighting the ribbons to prevent them from completely obscuring the rear windshield and backseat windows, would have been hilarious. Under these circumstances, Kristin cried. I turned up the radio.

Our next stop was a cake shop specializing in one-of-a-kind custom decorated cakes; behind the counter hung countless photographs of all kinds of celebrities with cakes sculpted to look like dinosaurs and dogs and even pizza, commemorating twenty-first birthdays, film premieres, album releases, and any other milestone you could think of. We picked up a gigantic sheet cake printed with edible photographs from Season 3: one of Buffy with Angel and one of Buffy with Faith (the other person she sure seems to spend a lot of time with during this era of the show). It read, HAPPY PROM CLASS OF 1999. Back in the car again, we fought. At every stop, we put on our public faces and were cordial until we'd completed the task at hand. Then we'd get back into the car and pick up the fight right where we'd left off.

Things were not ideal, and it's very possible we made them more fraught in our efforts to make them feel less so. It was certainly "everybody act casual!" thinking that led us to share a hotel room—first to get dressed for the dance, and later to sleep in the same bed, even though we hadn't done that in weeks. But once the prep work was completed (I beg of you to envision your soon-to-be ex-wife crying at you in a parking lot while you bat back dozens of balloons), we resolved, for the sake of our listeners, to put on a happy face worthy of prom night.

As usual, our kids[6] made all of the discomfort and weirdness worth it, a thousand times over. Highlights from the evening included *Buffering* songs as well as select nineties hits; a

---

6 Our listeners, who lovingly refer to us as Pod-Mom (Kristin) and Pod-Dad (Jenny).

handful of special guest vocalists; an unplanned dance-off be-tween two queer Spike cosplayers (the cheers from the crowd rivaled those from many a boy band concert); custom choco-lates made by our friends at Lagusta's Luscious in the shapes of coffins and anatomical hearts; a dance playlist featuring songs by Britney, *NSYNC, Fatboy Slim, and Spice Girls (no songs released after 1999 allowed!); a handmade photo booth with a backdrop of Sunnydale's colors of maroon and gold; and a punch fountain that, by the end of the night, featured a hand-drawn sign that said SPIKED.

There are two immensely memorable moments in *Buffy*'s "The Prom" episode. She has gone to prom alone, just days after Angel has told her that he is leaving town and does not plan to return. Buffy has spent three years battling back vampires, demons, and all manner of evil to keep her fellow students protected, all in secret. However, she learns at prom that although her classmates may not understand the specifics, they have seen her and have understood her to be the person who has kept them safe.

Jonathan, a classmate of the Scoobies, stands at a micro-phone onstage to read a speech to Buffy and present her with an unexpected award. He says:

> *Whenever there was a problem or something creepy happened, you seemed to show up and stop it. Most of the people here have been saved by you or helped by you at one time or another. We're proud to say that the Class of '99 has the lowest mortality rate of any graduating class in Sunnydale history, and we know at least part of that is because of you.*

At our prom in Los Angeles, a collection of our listeners similarly took the mic to present us with something we did not expect. This collection of *Buffering* Scoobies had adapted

Jonathan's speech to reflect their feelings for us and the *Buffer-ing* community, and had made us an award to mirror the exact award given to Buffy in 1999: a golden parasol.

Buffy's award had read, BUFFY SUMMERS, CLASS PROTEC-TOR, and on ours there was a handwritten plaque that said, JENNY AND KRISTIN, CLASS PROTECTORS.

Our whole, entire hearts.

For Buffy, the other massive moment in "The Prom" happens at the very end of the episode. For better or for worse, Angel has donned a tuxedo and has come to say goodbye to Buffy. The song that plays as they hold each other close on the dance floor is the Sundays' cover of "Wild Horses."

At our prom, this *was* a moment we'd anticipated. I was going to perform the song for the last dance, and Kristin and I would have to be in a room of wall-to-wall Scoobies who knew us as a couple while I sang about a love so strong that those it was shared between could not be torn apart by the most powerful forces.

When we'd talked about this moment leading up to prom night, Kristin had said she would have to leave the room. How was she supposed to stand there and listen to this song, the same song that Buffy and Angel had danced to before it all came to a crashing end for them? How could she watch me sing these same words while she stood alone, knowing what was coming once the night was over?

As I strummed the song's opening chords, though, our listeners formed a circle on the dance floor, arms over shoulders, holding each other close. They knew nothing of what was happening to both of us then, but still beckoned to Kristin to come and join them. They swayed together and sang along to the song, holding her when she needed it more than they could have ever imagined; holding her when *I* needed them to more than they could have ever imagined.

ENEMIES

I can't really say I never trusted you
That wouldn't be right but
How can anybody feel close to you
Indefinitely
Never go looking for what you can't find
It doesn't feel right but
I guess we're going separate ways tonight

How could you and me, you and me
Ever be ever be enemies
You and me, you and me
I thought you and me, you and me
Could never be never be enemies
You and me, you and me

I can't really figure out where we went wrong
I should have said something else
Maybe I could have done some of these things
Differently
Couldn't handle half a dose
    of you being so stone cold
Thought I was invincible
But I was wrong

How could you and me, you and me
Ever be ever be enemies
You and me, you and me
I thought you and me, you and me
Could never be never be enemies
You and me, you and me

I can't really say I never trusted you
How can anybody feel close to you

How could you and me, you and me
Ever be ever be enemies
You and me, you and me
I thought you and me, you and me
Could never be never be enemies
You and me, you and me

chapter four

THE HARSH LIGHT OF DAY

When the smoke clears after graduation day, the surviving members of Sunnydale's class of '99 (that is, those who were neither exsanguinated by vampires nor devoured by a post-ascension-yet-pre-explosion Giant Demon Snake Mayor during the ceremony) have taken that momentous step over the threshold from childhood into adulthood. But the transition from high school to whatever comes next is pretty much always tumultuous for the person going through it, and Buffy is no exception.

And while acclimating to college (or perhaps more accurately, acclimating to life after high school), Buffy must continue her fight against evil.

There's the quintessential UC Sunnydale "mean girl"—as it happens, a powerful coed vampire—who leaves some serious dents in both Buffy's confidence and her body. There's the "roommate from hell" who clips her toenails in the common space, labels each individual hard-boiled egg that belongs to her in their shared minifridge, and blasts Cher's "Believe" on repeat, while also *literally* sucking away parts of Buffy's soul, little by little each night. And there's Parker, the smooth talker who helps Buffy check off the "guy who sleeps with you and then never calls you again" square on her College Freshman

Bingo card (bonus points if you later catch him using the exact same line he used on you—involving his dead mother!!!—on some other girl).

Meanwhile, her friends are taking their own tentative steps out of high school and into the world beyond. Willow begins to dive more deeply into witchcraft. Xander forgoes college entirely and enters the workforce, drifting from one dead-end job to the next. Even Giles, who is no longer Buffy's Watcher and is without a library to tend, is teetering on the verge of a midlife crisis. The whole Scooby gang seems trapped in a Spearsian paradox: not a girl, not yet a woman. Thus, in addition to adjusting to college and continuing her ongoing battle against the forces of darkness, Buffy also finds herself with less of a support system—the very thing that has set her apart from Slayers past and likely lengthened her life expectancy.

Buffy's attempts to adjust to her new normal are overwhelmed by the reality that life never slows down—especially for a Slayer.

If high school was hell, college is all nine circles.

I thought I knew what I was getting into
Took a deep breath, leapt out of the window

Kristin

When we woke up the morning after prom, everything was right where we'd left it. We'd shared a room—and a bed—for the first time in weeks, and waking up next to each other was more of a reminder of the chasm between us than anything else. Looking at Jenny that morning felt like knowing every cell of her in the same exact breath as not knowing her at all. Like a panic attack left on the stovetop overnight to reduce.

Luckily, there was more vampiric distraction afoot. We'd invited promgoers (and the many folks who hadn't been able to get tickets) to join us for a casual hangout and sing-along at Griffith Park the morning after prom. So we got up, dragged ourselves out of our respective doom spirals, got dressed, and drove to the meetup spot: a grassy knoll encircled by tall shade trees and speckled with picnic tables.

Dozens of Scoobies were there waiting for us and, just as it had the night before, being in their presence lightened the heaviness of our hearts for the following two hours. Jenny had brought her acoustic guitar, and folks gathered in a circle around the two of us. Jenny played *Buffering* songs while I held up lyrics on my phone for her to read and everyone sang along.

When we left the park later that afternoon, the weight of it all came back in waves. We went out to a late lunch, just the two of us. In the car later that night, I overenthusiastically explained to Jenny my most recent discoveries about our marriage—the many ways I could single-handedly make it better, be a better partner, get it *right*, if we just had a little more time. Please. Please. Please.

We were just a few episodes away from completing our coverage of Season 3, and after many long conversations riddled with tears, anger, confusion, and exhaustion, we decided that we'd army-crawl through our last few recordings and then take two months off from the podcast before returning with Season 4. At the time, neither of us could imagine how we'd ever be able to continue, but we also had no way of envisioning a world where we stopped. Making a plan—even if it was foolish, even if we didn't believe it—was something to hold on to as we began to sort out how to untangle our shared life, both privately and publicly.

Even though there was an entire broken life demanding my attention in Los Angeles, three days after dancing the night away at our first *Buffy* Prom I left to be with my closest friends in Brooklyn.

If only we'd consulted the *Buffy* mirror in which we increasingly saw our lives reflected, we could have glimpsed our futures. If Buffy was going to have to adjust to a whole new life without a break from saving the world, we were going to have to adjust to our new lives without a break from our work (or each other).

On my flight from Los Angeles to New York, I opened an email inviting us to appear as special guests at an event called the Vampire Ball happening that winter in London. The more I read, the more I could not believe what I was reading: we were being offered roundtrip airfare, lodging, and a talent fee to join some of the most beloved actors from *Buffy*—including James Marsters (Spike), Juliet Landau (Drusilla), and Mark Metcalf (the Master, a.k.a. Mr. Fruit Punch Mouth)—to participate in signings and photo sessions *with* the cast, *and* to do a live taping of the podcast for all of the attendees.[1]

The idea of flying to London months from that moment seemed absolutely absurd. Would the podcast even still exist by December? Would we still be *speaking* to one another in December? The idea of *not* flying to London seemed equally ridiculous; how could we turn down one of the most magical offers we'd ever received?

Failing almost instantly at our plan to take space from each

---

1 For more on our favorite interactions with the cast of *Buffy*, see Appendix B!

other, I picked up my phone—what else could I do!!—and texted Jenny from thirty thousand feet: "Hey, so."

In the conversation that followed, we set a ground rule that would inform many of our choices in the months to come: when offered an opportunity we would say yes, we would hope for the best (for a miracle, truly), and then when the moment arrived to do the thing we'd said yes to, we would see if we could actually do it.

Mere days after we'd sent our first hopeful yes to the good folks at the Vampire Ball, *Time* magazine released their list of the top podcasts of 2018. There we were: *Buffering the Vampire Slayer*. A few weeks after that, *Esquire* released their own list of best podcasts of the year. There we were *again*: *Buffering the Vampire Slayer*. Our listenership soared; these were the biggest accolades our work had ever received, all arriving at the exact moment of our deepest pain.

From the moment our separation began (and no matter how hard we tried to make it otherwise), we were in constant contact.

✴ ✴ ✴

I spent most of that spring getting on planes to various cities where close friends would house me and offer me the comforts of late-night glasses of wine, beds covered in soft blankets, and long dinners at my favorite restaurants. Jenny remained at our Altadena house, continuing her writing sessions and making sure that Sam stayed alive and well. When I would come back through Los Angeles, Jenny would leave to stay with her friends, who, I imagine, offered her similar comforts. At the start of April, we told our parents. Our parents who had walked us down the aisle on our wedding day, our parents who had celebrated our joys and shared in our losses, our parents who'd mailed us birthday gifts to open together with them on FaceTime from across the country, our parents who loved us and our love nearly as much as we had ourselves. For over a year, Jenny's mom had been planning a trip to visit us, which was scheduled for late April. We had to ask her to cancel it.

So now our closest friends knew. Our families knew. Our listenership, though, did not. Our fourth season was set to begin at the end of May, and we were terrified of breaking *their* hearts with the news. How do you tell thousands of people who have looked to your partnership as a beacon of hope that it is ending? How do you tell them everything is going to be okay when you're miles away from a place where you can believe that yourself?

We decided to take a three-pronged (and some might say unhinged) approach:

1. On May 23, return to *Buffering* with the Season 4 premiere, "The Freshman."
2. On May 24, announce an upcoming event—a live recording of "Beer Bad"—scheduled for July at Brooklyn's Littlefield.
3. On May 25, publish a statement announcing our separation.

We reasoned that, if our listeners saw that we would be together in NYC in July, then maybe they would be able to believe us when we told them it was going to be okay. I am pretty sure that we also reasoned: if we planned a show in July, then maybe . . . *we* would be okay.

We decided we should be together when the statement went live and so, sitting side by side—having read and reread the words, rewritten them, rearranged them, copyedited them—we hit Publish.

As some of you already know, we have been moving through a difficult time over the past few months. We live a complicated life where a lot of our personal experiences are public, and we feel very thankful for that in many ways because of how it connects us to all of you. We have spent the past nine years in each other's lives, and the past five years married. We have been through so much together, including creating a podcast which has grown a community that astounds us every day.

Over the past several months we have uncovered a difficult truth which we know will be surprising to many of you, as it was surprising to both of us. We've come to realize that we will be better—both to ourselves and to each other—within the context of a friendship, rather than a marriage.

One of our top priorities as we move through our separation is continuing to cultivate the beautiful community that has been created by *Buffering the Vampire Slayer*. While we know that there have been and will be bumps along the way, we have every intention of continuing to produce *Buffering* together. We have been privately moving through this for several months, and your collective love has been much of what has supported us. There will undoubtedly be some temporary structural changes as we work to heal the parts that hurt the most, but we are still here, and we are still with you all.

We also know that queer love is a very powerful thing to witness. With that in mind, we want you all to understand that our love was and is still powerful, that we still care very deeply for one another, and that our split will not change that fundamental truth.

We know that you will respect our privacy during this difficult time, and appreciate you all the more for it.

All our love,
Kristin & Jenny

We turned the comments off. We turned our phones off. We, incredibly, decided that we would go out and get our nails done. We left the nail salon and went out to dinner together at one of our favorite local spots. Absolutely nothing made sense.

We received an outpouring of emails—folks were kind, they were gentle, and they let us have more space than we'd dared to hope for, even from these, the most compassionately wonderful listeners a podcast could ever dream of having.

Jenny

I have always been a more private person than Kristin. The idea of posting an announcement to update a teeming, faceless internet-at-large about our relationship status, while second nature to her, elicited an immediate and unbidden response of discomfort from my core. Still, as much as I dreaded it, I knew it had to be done; we wanted to prepare our listeners for any potential bumps that might be waiting for us down the road as we attempted to keep our shared passion project alive in the face of our incredibly painful separation. Our friend Gabe, who had recently gone through a public-facing split, gave us some advice that made the whole idea a little easier to swallow: "Turn off the comments." Making the announcement a one-way transmission eased my apprehension . . . not completely, but enough.

The post was a bell that couldn't be unrung. Texts began to pour in from people in my life whom I hadn't yet told. I answered variations of the same questions again and again.

The more you say something, the more real it becomes.

We don't remember much from the weeks that followed. New podcast episodes aired. New songs were written. We lived apart, time-sharing the Altadena house and taking turns couch surfing, each of us staying up late to hash and rehash and re-rehash the details of our separation with the friends who hosted us during this period. We would get together to record things. Kristin, at some point, decided that she was moving back to Brooklyn. We told our landlord, who actually lived in the other half of our house, that we would be moving out at the start of August. She was more upset than anyone else we told, some-how, having gone through a painful divorce herself. She sat with Kristin in our living room one night and told her that we shouldn't do it; we were both good people, we should make it work. When Kristin relayed this to me, hot tears unexpectedly pricked the corners of my eyes. After our landlord had ended her own marriage, she'd divided her beautiful home into two apartments. From the light fixtures to the tile in the kitchen, every detail in the house felt handpicked, a choice made by someone who truly cared. This very kind woman had chosen us, had trusted us to be tenants in a space that clearly meant a great deal to her. It stung to feel like we were letting her down.

Operating true to "bite off more than could ever be chewed" form, we'd decided not only to launch a new season, announce a live event, *and* tell all of the internet that we were moving through divorce but also to launch a sister podcast covering the *Buffy* spinoff series, *Angel*.[2] Our plan for this second project, called *Angel on Top*, was to produce the podcast while two of our wonderfully talented friends—Brittany Ashley and Laura Zak, whose podcast cohosting chemistry had already been established on their *Daria* rewatch show *Sicker Sadder World*—would come on to host.

That July, we flew together to John F. Kennedy Airport for our "Beer Bad" event in Brooklyn. We still didn't know how to occupy space together; after nearly a decade, being partners was so ingrained in the way our bodies moved that in those first months, we'd always find ourselves either too far apart or too close. Being back in our home city for the first time without being a couple felt stranger than either of us had anticipated. Kristin cried as we moved toward the baggage claim area, and I instinctively squeezed her shoulder from behind as we rode the escalator down. I don't think it made either of us feel any better.

We stayed at separate friends' houses in Brooklyn, but I made my way to where Kristin was staying to supervise as she ironed fuzzy letters onto T-shirts that we would wear onstage for our live taping. Mine read, I LOVE HUNKS, and Kristin's said, FUCK OFF PARKER.[3]

While unpacking on the evening before our show, I made

---

2 After prom, Angel stays true to his word and leaves Sunnydale, moving to Los Angeles, where he opens a detective agency that specializes in investigating the paranormal and "helping the helpless." Detective Angel!

3 Our listeners had been tracking my love of hunks since practically the dawn of the podcast, but the intensity skyrocketed with the Season 4 arrival of my *favorite Buffy*verse hunk, Riley Finn. Similarly, note had been taken that if there was a man doing shitty things, Kristin would unleash fiery hellfury toward him instantaneously.

the kind of shocking discovery I could only imagine occurring while in a state of sleep-deprived emotional chaos such as the one I was currently moving through: I had neglected to pack a single pair of underwear. Socks? Check! T-shirts, including extras "just in case"?[4] You bet! But no matter how many times I took everything out of my suitcase and then carefully replaced it piece by piece, underwear failed to appear. It was too late in the evening for anything to be done about it until the following morning, at which time I zoomed out to obtain replacements. The next step was tricky and time sensitive, however. Currently without laundry facilities, but harboring a strong desire to launder new underwear prior to wearing, I hand-washed the garments in the bathroom sink and hung them to dry. As the clock ticked closer and closer to showtime, the boxer briefs remained stubbornly damp. I spent a solid half hour toasting them with a hairdryer—trying to call to mind various breathing exercises while fighting tears that were definitely *not* a reaction to my missing underwear—until finally they could be safely donned.

We arrived at Littlefield (I in a state of supreme toastiness) to a show that, just like every show we'd done since our Union Hall show in 2016 and every show we'd do for the run of the podcast, was sold out. Seating was first come, first served, and this resulted in a line snaking down Sackett Street in Brooklyn, wrapping around to Fourth Avenue. While "Beer Bad" is certainly not the crown jewel of the series, or even of the fourth season, it is a delightful episode that was made all the more enjoyable by drinking beer with our audience (on theme!), and with a very fun pod-detour in which we discussed the history of women in beer making (and their connection to the imagery traditionally associated with witches!).

---

4 Just in case *what*, exactly?!

We'd made a habit of hanging out at the merch table after our live shows, giving us the opportunity to high-five and take photos with folks who'd come out to see us. The combination of recent events and a sold-out show meant that we wound up speaking to audience members for over two hours, one and two at a time—nearly all of them sharing with us ways in which the podcast as a whole, or the two of us together, had helped them through various life circumstances. It was beautiful, and in our current emotionally compromised state, it was also exhausting.

Right before we got to the very end of the line, someone pulled Kristin aside. I was deep in conversation with another attendee, gesturing wildly to them about something that was probably related to Buffy bonking Parker over the head with a big stick.[5] This person, whom we'd never met, had come to the show with a message of a different tenor—one that Kristin would relay to me later that evening. He'd told her that he missed the show itself, but felt he had to come down to the venue simply to say that he'd believed in love until he learned we were separating—and now he didn't think love was real.

What can you possibly say to someone who has taken the noble, respectful efforts of hundreds of others and single-handedly smashed them to bits by making you feel exposed, vulnerable, and inexplicably judged for moving through heartbreak? As it turns out, you don't say anything at all. Through

---

5 In "Beer Bad," a warlock curses the campus bar's beer to reduce those who drink it to a Neanderthalesque state. CaveBuffy rescues Parker from a burning building, just as she would in her normal Slayer frame of mind. But then she does something decidedly un-Slayerlike; the magical loophole provided by cursed beer gives Buffy over to her base impulses and allows distinctly human justice to be served. She bonks him over the head with a big stick. Twice.

tears, Kristin told me that she had simply smiled,[6] nodded, and walked away.

It was a soul-crushing way to end the evening, and we both carried that with us as we packed up our merch and left. We were fully depleted. I flew back to LA the day after the show, and Kristin returned a few days later.

Kristin

Twilight's Edward and Bella have no place here—inside a story about Buffy and two girls who held tight to her baby-blue coat-tails as their lives split down the center—but in the summer of 2018 I did feel a bit like the heartbroken, cliff-jumping, motorcycle-riding, *New Moon*–era Bella Swan. New York City is my home, the singular city that has helped to hold *all* of my broken hearts over the decades, and when I left LA after *Buffy* Prom, I crash-landed into NYC's arms with a mission to do anything and everything I could think of to forget the devastation I had waiting for me back in California. Though admittedly I did not ride a motorcycle or jump off any (literal) cliffs, nothing that I did made me forget.

At first, my trips to New York were only intended as temporary reprieves from it all—a balm to soothe my hurts before returning back home for another round of emotional blows. The longer I was there, though, the more a new reality became clear: I could not stay in Los Angeles. I had never wanted to *go* to Los Angeles in the first place; I was born in New York, I had always lived in New York, and in my earliest conversations with Jenny about moving west I had asked her,

---

6 If this were a podcast, the Patriarchy jingle would play *very* loudly here.

through sobs, how I could ever be myself in a city like Los Angeles. "One of the biggest parts of who I am is being *angry* about New York City—my beloved, dirty, wretched, perfect city," I said across the little table in our long, narrow Brooklyn kitchen. "What if I am just *happy* about California? Who would I even *be*!?"

Though I'm proud that I ultimately returned and held true to my New York roots, Los Angeles never really got a fair shot. It was a city that, at first, made me feel isolated solely because of its newness, and then became the place where I'd felt even *more* alone as I sunk deeper and deeper into my body's inability to become pregnant. In its final act, it became the city where my marriage had shattered.

It took me longer to realize that I needed to move back to New York than it probably should have because I could not fathom the idea of leaving Jenny. I was nowhere close to being able to imagine a life where I didn't wake up next to her every day, let alone a life where we lived three thousand miles away from each other. When I finally told Jenny my plan, she was encouraging. She meant to make me feel *supported* by telling me that New York City would be good for me and that she understood, but of course it only broke my heart all over again that she didn't beg me to stay.

So now it was time to pack up our home.

We packed separately, in shifts—never together when items were divided and boxed up. For reasons I could not explain, I started the entire process of packing in the kitchen with the spices. We had two containers of cinnamon, so I guess at least the math made sense. One for me, one for Jenny. We had two spatulas, too. Jenny would take the record player. I would take the speakers. Jenny would take the pots and pans. I took the silverware. We divided the sheets. I took our bed. Jenny took the mattress from the guest room. I made the saddest spread-sheet in the entire world to keep track of our progress and our divisions.

I invited a few friends over to help me host a moving sale. In retrospect, I can't imagine why I didn't just donate anything we weren't taking with us to save myself from the pain of sitting in a driveway amidst the remains of my marriage, selling things for one dollar or two dollars apiece. We tried to sell a few of the larger items of furniture, one being the massive shipping pallet that we'd used as a coffee table since we'd been together. It had a large iron wheel in its center and smaller iron wheels on each side; I had purchased it when I had my first "real job" and had lugged all three hundred pounds of it to four apartments in Brooklyn and two houses in California. Neither of us could bear the thought of moving it a sixth time, but as our moving day got closer and closer, it still had not sold. In the end, I had to give it away for free. I cried at our dining-room window watching as two men heaved it onto their truck bed and drove away.

Cruelly, the last episode Jenny and I were set to record together before we moved out of our home was "Wild at Heart," in which Willow and Oz break up. Oz, who has been in a relationship with Willow for the past two seasons, finds connection with another—a fellow werewolf named Veruca. In the conflict that results after this revelation, Oz realizes that he needs to figure some things out about himself, and he needs to do that alone. He packs and leaves town at the end of the episode, telling Willow she is the only person he ever loved.

Now, we are *incredible* compartmentalizers . . . but this was too much life imitating art, even for us.

So I picked up the phone. And Joanna Robinson—friend, podcaster, savior—answered.

I asked if she'd sub in for Jenny as my cohost on this heartbreaking episode.[7]

An emphatic yes.

A podcast-saving yes.

After I'd hung up with Joanna, I couldn't stop thinking about Willow. Looking out the window, through the dark, to the tree that bordered the driveway of a house that no longer felt like home, my brain began to whirl. What if this episode's song was from Willow's perspective? What if I wrote down what *I* was feeling as my world came apart, and we put those words into Willow's voice as she watched Oz drive his van out of Sunnydale?

I picked up my phone again, opened a blank email, and began to write. The words came out in a rush. We'd decided before the start of the season that Jenny should take over songwriting entirely—affording us a small measure of space from one another—but I couldn't help myself. This was Willow's song, but it was also mine. I sent the email to Jenny, asking her if she could use some of my words for Willow's lyrics, before I fell asleep.

---

7 Months before, I'd prepared Joanna for this moment, taking her out for dinner in New York to one of my favorite spots in the city. Tucked in an actual alley off Rivington Street on the Lower East Side, Freemans Alley has some magical, time-portal aesthetic going on—flickering candles, worn wooden tables, a quiet warmth. Joanna often describes that dinner as "the night one of my parents told me that they were divorcing," a nod to the shared nature of our friendship with Joanna and the way I opened the conversation once we'd been seated: "There is something I have to tell you."

Much of what I'd written made its way into the final lyrics of the song, and Jenny wrote a melody that was as beautiful as it was gutting. I am not a musician, and while I love unlocking lyrics with Jenny, she is the only one of us who can manifest a *song*. I have always envied those who can take their hurt and shape it into music, and hearing my words inside the melody she'd crafted felt closer than I'd ever imagined I would get to having that experience myself. Our good friend Bess Rogers entered the *Buffering* universe as the voice of Willow.

The final version of the song begins:

How can you leave me?
How can you go?
What were we, even?
I used to know

A Note from Jenny

When Kristin asked me to shape her words into lyrics I was initially hesitant, in part because Kristin generally left the sad songs to me and in part because I wasn't anywhere near ready to read what Kristin needed to write. But I took a deep breath and decided to try. I took Kristin's words, written to be sung from the perspective of Willow, and set them to music. It was the only time in the seven-season run that we'd create a song this way, and to my surprise it came together quite naturally. I knew that this moment in Willow's arc was resonating deeply with Kristin, and I knew from years of experience the powerful catharsis offered by the act of writing music from a place of pain. Giving her the space to write the lyrics, and supporting those lyrics by building the melody and harmonic movement around the words, felt like a small act of service, a tiny helpful thing I was able to do for her during a time when it seemed like everything I did just hurt her more.

Early Lyric Ideas for "Wild at Heart"
From: Kristin
Date: Tue, Jul 17, 2018 at 10:49 PM
Subject: Willow Song
To: Jenny
These are just streams of consciousness. I'd love to hear melody thoughts and anything else before it gets too underway.

How can you leave me
How can you go
What were we, even?
How can you know

I trusted you
I trusted us
My heart's center cannot hold
Was it real?
Where will you go?
I thought I was your anchor
I thought I was your guiding force
How could anything break us
What have you done?
Where will I go?

Here if you have questions before beginning.

Sent from my iPhone

WILD AT HEART

How can you leave me?
How can you go?
What were we, even?
I used to know

My heart, my center, oh it cannot hold
Was it ever real? Where will I go?

How can you leave me?
How can you go?
What were we, even?
Did I ever know?

I was your lighthouse here to guide you home
Without your north star, now where will you go?

I thought you'd hold me, keep me safe from harm
But now I'm broken and you feel so far
I thought you'd hold me, keep me safe from harm
But now I'm broken

How can you leave me?
How can you go?
What were we, even?
Did I ever know?

How can you leave me?
How can you go?
What were we, even?
I'll never know

Jenny

Before Kristin left town to move into her new Brooklyn apartment, we met up for one last dinner together (yes, at the same spot we'd had dinner after our divorce announcement, because we love closing a loop). Afterward, I walked Kristin back to her temporary residence—an apartment that belonged to neither of us—and, once inside, we wondered what was left to do. I held Sam. We both cried. We stood at the kitchen sink. We hugged each other tightly. And then I walked out the front door.

In the morning, Kristin and Sam flew across the country to start the next chapter of their lives without me.

＋.＊.˙✕˙

After she moved back east, Kristin and I didn't see each other in person again until four months later, when I flew to New York in advance of our trip to London for the Vampire Ball.

Since our initial yes to the invitation had somehow, against all odds, remained a yes, we did what we always do: we added more to our plates. We scheduled an ice cream social—certainly unseasonable with regard to the wintry weather in Brooklyn, but timely, as it coincided with our coverage of the *Buffy-Angel* crossover episode "I Will Remember You."

A quick rundown for those who have forgotten: Buffy visits Angel in Los Angeles, he becomes (briefly) human, and the temporarily reunited couple shares (among many other things) a pint of ice cream. We were mystified by the flavor that Angel excitedly scarfs down: cookie dough fudge mint chip. Our research revealed that this flavor mash-up is not offered by any standard ice cream maker; thus, we ordered a custom batch of this fictional varietal from a company that specializes in turning your ice cream dreams into ice cream realities, and invited our local listeners to come share a scoop with us at Mission Dolores in Park Slope. Should we tell you that the last time we were there together was for the after-party following our wedding reception? At this point, *why even bother?*

I was staying in town through the Thanksgiving holiday to do some music-related work, and since Kristin would be up-state with her family, we had the brilliant, money-saving idea for me to stay at Kristin's new Brooklyn apartment with Sam.

My birthday occasionally falls on Thanksgiving, and this fact, in combination with a career that demands a great deal of travel, has yielded some fairly depressing ghosts of birthdays past. The number one saddest year up to this point involved a Thanksgiving Day + birthday dinner consisting of vending machine waffles eaten alone in a Belgian hotel room at around 1 A.M. I never expected that year would be knocked out of the top slot, but I also never expected I'd one day be staying by my-self in my ex-wife's apartment on my thirty-seventh birthday, with my cat who was no longer my cat, eating packaged soup from a bag for Thanksgiving dinner.

I left New York for London ahead of Kristin to do some songwriting while I was in town. In my experience, most co-writing sessions begin with a sort of introductory period, per-haps an hour or so, which you might spend getting to know more about the other writers, whom there's a decent chance you've only just met. It's not uncommon to cover where you're from, what you've been listening to, and the bloody, intimate details of whatever deeply personal crisis you might currently be enduring. Over the years, I had grown accustomed to fostering space within a session for the emotional purging of other writers; circumstances now being what they were, I suddenly found myself in the hot seat, attempting to sift any potential lyrical gold from the muck and mire of my current emotional evisceration for the good of the writing sessions. This constant prodding of open wounds cultivated a general rawness that made even simple, decidedly unsad things feel very charged, and sometimes unbearable.

A couple of days into my London stay, I had to switch hotels, moving to the one where the Vampire Ball was being hosted. That morning after checking out, I took an Uber to a session in a sweet residential neighborhood, carrying along two suitcases, a guitar, a backpack, and a phone that suddenly refused to dial UK phone numbers. This wouldn't have been a problem except that none of the adorable houses seemed to have street numbers on them; I had no idea where I was supposed to go. Unable to call the gentlemen with whom I was scheduled to write and ask them just where the heck they were located, I lugged my gear up and down the street looking for house numbers, or someone to ask for directions, or perhaps a building that looked like a music studio, all to no avail. A couple of blocks down from the spot where I'd been dropped off, I found what appeared to be a business of some kind and knocked on the door. By the time a woman came outside, I had cracked; the normally tolerable experiences of lugging a lot of stuff around, being lost, and having phone trouble gained power in combination, and then filtered through the prism of Divorce Business to create white-hot unbearability, until the only thing left to do was cry. After I explained the circumstances through a combination of gestures and monosyllabic yelps between sobs, the woman let me borrow her cell phone. I called my soon-to-be collaborators and they graciously promised to come outside into the street and look extremely conspicuous until I found them.

That day I met Jacob Attwooll and Matt Zara for the first time and wrote "Merry Go Round," which I'd release several years later:

the faded blur how do you fight it
took all you have to just survive it
the color drains and you're reminded:
try to keep your head and try to like it

it's hard to know when you can't see it
the shadows lined with words you keep in
the ghosts you hold the salt you're breathing
we'll make it real or else we'll make-believe it

+ .+. .*.

Despite the hell of it all, the Vampire Ball was a very special experience. We got to hang in the green room with Spike/ James, Drusilla/Juliet, and the Master/Mark, as well as other members of the cast. James talked with us about the capacity of genre storytelling to hold ideas much broader than the material. Mark asked Kristin about her use of the word "queer," which led to a larger conversation about the reclamation of that specific word and the never-ending evolution of language. Brian Thompson, who pulled double duty as Luke in the series pilot and the Judge in the second season, took an interest in the musical component of the podcast and asked me how many songs I'd written in my life up to that point. He told me he loved to play piano but had only ever written one song, which he'd played at the funeral of a close friend. The whole time we couldn't believe that it was all just . . . so normal.

We did a live taping of Season 4's "This Year's Girl," we participated in a Q+A panel, we signed posters, and we took photographs with listeners—including a very sweet baby named Pippa, the youngest Scooby we had ever met. We were almost always surrounded by cast members and convention attendees, and our public faces were pretty much constantly on, despite the continuing discomfort beneath the surface.

In the unavoidable moments when we *were* alone, though, the thorns came poking through. The night before the convention began, we arranged an extracurricular pub meetup with our listeners in Kew Gardens. It was a rowdy good time, and we got to have a pint with folks who couldn't make it to the con, or who just wanted some extra hang time.[8] When the gathering wound down, Kristin and I stepped out into the night, which was cold and quiet compared with the busy pub. We walked around the neighborhood looking for a place to eat, eventually settling on a restaurant with the general atmosphere of an English hunting lodge. I mourned the traditional restaurant seating convention that placed us on opposite sides

---

8 This meetup was also vital to the completion of the song for Season 4, Episode 13: "The I in Team." I had not been able to complete the recording before flying to London, and thus had traveled with a mobile recording rig. Unfortunately, I didn't account for this when packing, and when I set up my recording gear in the London hotel, I found myself short one US-to-UK power adapter. Thankfully, our listeners came to the rescue and someone brought a loaner adapter to the pub! I was able to complete the recording in my hotel room later that night.

of the table, facing one another. There was no escaping the discomfort . . . which only intensified as Kristin began to tell me about an essay she was writing about our miscarriage and divorce.

As I mentioned earlier, I'm not wild about the nooks and crannies of my personal life being made public. Perhaps this reads as counterintuitive, as some of my most private thoughts live inside dozens of songs that I have written and released for public consumption. However, though my music is extremely personal, my approach to making it has always been rooted in *storytelling*. Sometimes those stories are mine, sometimes they belong to others, and sometimes they're entirely made up; most often they are probably some combination of the three. Any way you slice it, there is metaphor and figurative language in play, creating a comfortable force field of plausible deniability. I find this invaluable in the pursuit of coexisting alongside the things that I create.[9]

An essay written by my ex-wife—about a time when we were married and enduring great pain—was a different beast entirely.

And yet.

When you go through a miscarriage, you learn that they are very common. At first this might sound purely terrible, and it is—I would not wish the loss of a pregnancy on my greatest enemy. But what made the worst day of my life feel a tiny bit less awful was the discovery that we were far less alone than the world would have us believe. This is what settled my heart with regard to Kristin writing about our loss. She had spent years using her words to bring light, laughter, and hope

---

9 Kristin can confirm that she had to wrestle me to the ground and pull every last detail from me, like so many teeth, for this memoir.

to LGBTQ young people and their families, and I knew that now she could bring some light into the hearts of people going through their darkest hour. I wasn't able to say any of this at the time; I am known in some circles for my uncomfortable silences. Kristin knows me though, so it is likely she understood even then that I recognized the importance of what she was working on. When she sent me the essay a few days before it was published, although I bristled at paragraphs that bumped up on the edges of our separation, I was able to tell her that what she wrote was beautiful and would be a balm on the souls of those who read it. I was able to tell her that I was proud of her.

On the last day of the convention, Kristin rang my hotel room first thing in the morning. "My body is starting to crumble," she said, going on to detail the sore throat, body aches, and impending sense of flu with which she had awoken. As you may have gathered by now, we are the kind of people who will simply power through any brand of apocalypse to keep our commitments, and flu-pocalypse was included on the list. This was a realm in which I knew what to do and how to help, no uncomfortable silences necessary! I immediately bolted to a nearby pharmacy, arriving at Kristin's door ten minutes later with an armload of medicine, tea, and other supplies to combat her symptoms. Our love for each other has always shone most brightly when circumstances allow Kristin to ask for help (something that is very hard for her to do) and allow me to provide the necessary care. In this, a time when we'd been thousands of miles apart in ways both literal and figurative, I was grateful to have been given a small, safe space to show her that I still cared for her and feel the love she still had for me in return.

We made it through our last day at the event and flew home; Kristin to New York, me to Los Angeles.

Both of Us

In the entirety of *Buffy*'s fourth season, we somehow managed to record all but three episodes together. Jenny would record "Where the Wild Things Are" with our friend Hrishikesh Hirway and "The Yoko Factor" with *Angel on Top* cohosts Brittany and Laura. Kristin recorded several other episodes with Joanna in an effort to take the space we felt we desperately needed . . . but without fail, we'd miss each other. We'd miss arguing about Riley, tracking the developing magic-as-queerness metaphor in the Tara and Willow love story,[10] unlocking new Hellmath theorems, and everything else—so after all that, we would end up rerecording the episodes together anyway.

We had planned our second *Buffy* Prom for the coming March, this time at the Ace Hotel in New York City. Our listeners presented us with handmade gifts onstage: a tiara for Kristin, a scepter for Jenny, and two lab coats with custom embroidery. Kristin's, a nod to the many times she'd shouted out particularly sexy dialogue between Buffy and Faith in Season 3, read, KRISTIN RUSSO, EROTIC POET LAUREATE. Jenny's, for reasons made clear already, read, JENNY OWEN YOUNGS, HUNKOLOGIST.

---

10 Once at college, Buffy's best pal Willow joins a Wicca group and meets Tara, who becomes both her spell buddy and her girlfriend. Due to the constraints imposed by Standards and Practices at the time, it would take a year for them to kiss on-screen. The writers tried to work around this by weaving a somewhat convoluted metaphor into the show, substituting various magical activities in place of anything overtly romantic between the two: floating a rose and plucking the petals off the bloom one by one, interlacing their fingers to build up the energy needed to move a vending machine, and performing a spell so powerful that upon its completion both witches are left lying on their backs panting and sweating. Gee, I wonder what that was meant to evoke!

Jenny sang *Buffering* songs mixed in with nostalgic covers of The Cranberries' "Linger" and "Kiss Me" by Sixpence None the Richer. Kristin crowd-surfed (a thing she had never done before and will likely never do again) when our prom DJ played the Violent Femmes' "Blister in the Sun." The night ended, as it had the previous year, with Jenny singing "Wild Horses" and our Scoobies swaying together, enveloping Kristin into the fold once more. This year, they knew much more about what we were going through, but the gesture seemed to be rooted in the same exact place as it had been the year prior: regardless of the circumstances, they simply cared about us.

Since that first prom in 2018, we'd recovered at least a little bit from the complete shock and upheaval of separating spices, saying goodbye to beloved pets, and putting three thousand miles of literal space between us. It was an ever-evolving kind of pain, and we still had to pretend the sadness and anger away when we found ourselves together without our shared work to lean on. But when we were in *Buffering* mode, things always felt easier. We knew who we were to others, even when we did not know who we were to each other.

This is the lesson that *Buffering* was teaching us, had been teaching us, and would keep teaching us. Sometimes, the work you do collides with your life and you feel like you're living inside all nine circles of hell. Sometimes, the work you do collides with your life and reminds you of who you are or—in the most powerful moments—shows you who you might be able to become.

THE HARSH LIGHT OF DAY

I thought I knew what I was getting into
Took a deep breath, leapt out of the window
Looking for an updraft, updraft
I didn't get to catch that, catch that

Will it always feel like this
Where it starts off with a kiss
Then leaves me licking my wounds
And thinking of you

Way back before I ever saw your face
I thought that love was something I should chase
I thought it'd fade but what do I know
I'm darker underneath your shadow

Will it always feel like this
Where it starts off with a kiss
Then leaves me licking my wounds
And thinking of you

I want to see the world without you
*   but I don't know if I'm able*
The demon in my bedside table
You left a mark on me that's feeling kind of fatal
The demon in my bedside table

Will it always feel like this
Where it starts off with a kiss
Then leaves me licking my wounds
And thinking of you

Our Most Important Contribution to the *Buffy* Conversation . . . and Also the World?!

When Faith Lehane first rolled into Sunnydale, we couldn't help but notice that all of a sudden things were feeling a little . . . *gay*? After this new Slayer arrives, things heat up *quickly*. Out of a sense of responsibility to our listenership and the larger queer community, we kept a watchful eye on this dynamic and made some startling discoveries.

Sure, we're not the first people to discuss the nearly canonical romance between Buffy and Faith; the ship name "Fuffy" existed long before Kristin ever watched the series! However, to our knowledge no one had ever sat down to prove, once and for all, that in the (allegedly) deleted scenes from the episode "Bad Girls," these two Slayers did in fact kick the proverbial gearshift.

Here, now printed and bound (making it official, actually), is our proof.

Date: February 8, 1999

Time: Sometime after dark

Location: One of Sunnydale's numerous cemeteries

Enter Buffy and her new pal Faith, out for an evening patrol. Faith is casually probing Buffy about her relationship with Xander while the pair engage in the synchronized slaying of NPC-grade vampires. When Buffy maintains that she and Xander are just friends, Faith counters, "What are friends for?" Good question, Faith.

During this exchange, Buffy also asserts that sex between pals ruins friendships . . . and you know what friendship is never the same after the following events? Buffy and Faith's.

Date: February 9, 1999

Time: Between the hours of 1 P.M. and 2 P.M. Pacific Standard Time

Location: Science class

Buffy sits with Xander and Willow, unable to stop herself from gushing about her new gal pal.

Speak of the devil and she shall appear! Faith saunters up outside the classroom, uses her breath to fog up the windowpane next to Buffy's desk, and then moves her finger through the fog to draw a heart and a stake piercing it. Flirt much?!

She bids Buffy to abandon her pop quiz and climb out the window for vampire adventures; there's a newly

hey girlfriend...

bad time?

discovered nest across town that needs to be erad-
icated! What can Buffy do but comply?

Buffy and Faith depart Sunnydale High together.
We are *generously* assuming that science class is the
final class of the day. The average US high school
completes the standard school day between 2 P.M. and
3 P.M.

Time: Between the hours of 2:30 P.M. and 4:00 P.M.
Pacific Standard Time
Location: A Sunnydale vamp nest

Buffy and Faith arrive at the nest of vampires,
ready to slay. Now, sure, there's no clock on the
wall of the crypt to show us the *exact* time, but
this town is like two blocks wide. Even if these
two "friends" were walking backward blindfolded,
it would take them, max, an hour to cross town.

When the door is kicked in by our heroic pair,
sunlight streams into the nest. Even without a
clock, it's clearly still daytime, *hours* from dusk.

Need more data? A Google search tells us the
sun set at 5:36 P.M. in Santa Barbara on February 9,
1999, the date this episode aired.[1]

Time: Late night, after hours Pacific Standard
Time
Location: The Bronze
We are confronted with Buffy and Faith *thrusting*,

---

1 Santa Barbara has long been established as the city that Sunnydale was most
closely based on, and it is also the city where nearly all of the exterior shots in
the show were filmed. See Appendix B for further discussion on this matter.

and *grinding,* and *tossing hair* with abandon on the dance floor at the Bronze. It is dark outside. The sun has *set.* It is *nighttime.*

Furthermore, *no one dances like this before 10 P.M.* NO ONE.

This gives us *at least* a *five-hour window* between the vamp-nest slayage and Thrust O'Clock, during which Faith and Buffy are unaccounted for.

SO, GENTLE READER: HOWEVER DID THEY PASS THE TIME?

Well-trusted lore tells us that Slayers get both hungry and horny after a good slay.[2] So perhaps they used some of the missing time to eat. Let's hypothesize:

- A muffin from the Espresso Pump would fill 20 minutes tops.
- Ribs at the Sunnydale Applebee's would take 60 minutes at most.
- A five-course lunch at the local white-tablecloth establishment? Still looking at a maximum of 120 minutes of chewing.

2 "Faith, Hope & Trick," *Buffy the Vampire Slayer,* Season 3, Episode 3, original air date October 1998.

This still leaves *a minimum of three hours* unaccounted for!

We think *you know* what they did in the time between.

We believe we've *proved* what they did in the time between.

Probably at the Sunnydale Motel, where it was great and they loved it and they want to do it again.

August, 2013: Giving them the ol' razzle dazzle on our wedding day at The Bell House. Eric Ryan Anderson

♡ The (Gay) Agenda ♡
5:00 The Witching Hour
5:30 Cocktails in the Lounge
6:30 Dinnertime
7:30 Champagne Toast followed by dancing
8:30 Larry & his Flask followed by dancing
10:00 You Don't Have to Go Home but you Can't Stay Here

August 2013: The (very gay) order of (very gay) events.
Eric Ryan Anderson

BOTTOM LEFT: December 2015: Kristin sits amidst all our belongings as we pack up our Brooklyn apartment.
All personal snapshots courtesy of the authors

BOTTOM RIGHT: December 2015: Only the Christmas tree remains on our last night at 223 Twenty-Seventh Street in Brooklyn before heading west to Los Angeles.

CLOCKWISE FROM TOP LEFT:

January 2016: Jenny's attempt at a Grand Canyon snowball, sixty years after her dad made one in the very same spot.

August 2016: Kristin sitting in our old green armchair, about to record our very first episode of *Buffering the Vampire Slayer*.

October 2016: Excitedly clutching the print copy of *Entertainment Weekly* in which *Buffering the Vampire Slayer* was featured on the "Must List" only a month after its debut.

March 2017: Decked out in our '90s finest before our very first live watch of *Buffy* with the Scoobies.

May 2017: A-Camp in Wisconsin, shortly before we drove the van to the Madison Emergency Room. Molly Adams

August 2017: Being very approachable at our booth at Flame Con in NYC.

October 2017: Our "Band Candy"–inspired Halloween costumes. Garage your police cars!

October 2017: Tiny Sam's contribution to our first Halloween cosplay, as the titular "Band Candy."

October 2017: Sam in our Altadena home with a custom *Buffering* "Awoooo" pumpkin carved by Jenny.

CKWISE FROM TOP LEFT:

cember 2017: Nerf Herder gifting us
iece of the actual Hellmouth.

arch 2018: Jenny spiraling into the
ss on her friend Molly's couch.

arch 2018: Some "Spike-d" *Buffy*
m punch at The Ace Hotel in Los
geles. Molly Adams

arch 2018: Prom pose at *Buffy* Prom
18. Molly Adams

TOP, LEFT, AND RIGHT:

December 2018: The whole gang from Vampire Ball in London. L-R: Kristin, Jenny, Tom Lenk, Ksenia Solo, James Marsters, Andrew J. Ferchland, Brian Thompson, Brody Hutzler, Juliet Landau, Marc Metcalfe.

April 2019: Outside of HeadGum Studios with the one and only Charisma Carpenter (Cordelia Chase).

April 2019: The Cheese Man himself, David Wells, being an awfully good sport with our sliced American cheese.

OPPOSITE PAGE TOP, LEFT, AND RIGHT:

March 2018: Holding our very own Class Protector award at *Buffy* Prom. Molly Adams

April 2018: Kristin and Harry Groener with a thing of beauty (boss) at our house in Altadena.

May 2018: Kristin taking a turtleneck time-out during a recording in our Altadena home studio.

CLOCKWISE LEFT TO RIGHT:

May 2019: Inside the Stoopid Buddy Studios photobooth with Seth Frickin' Green!

January 2019: After wrapping our interview with the brilliant James Marsters (Spike).

April 2019: Our second annual *Buffy* Prom at The Ace Hotel in NYC. Molly Adams

April 2019: Moments after receiving custom-made scepter and tiara from our beautiful Scoobies at *Buffy* Prom. Molly Adams

April 2019: Kristin's first (and certainly last) *Buffy* Prom crowd-surf. Molly Adams

CLOCKWISE FROM LEFT:

December 2019: Cosplaying as Boxer Rebellion Spike and Drusilla for our "Fool for Love" live taping in San Francisco.

December 2019: Jenny and Marc Blucas (Riley Finn) comparing hand sizes. (Marc won.)

October 2021: Photo assistant Frank being both helpful and professional at our annual Halloween costume photo shoot.

October 2021: Buffy *and* her tombstone?! Name a more iconic duo!

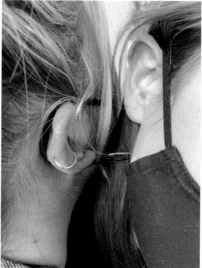

CLOCKWISE FROM LEFT:

March 2022: The universe spoke (and we listened) as Kristin's earring became inextricably entwined with Jess's mask strap.

March 2022: Jenny zooms in, cackling, while doing absolutely nothing to help her wife and ex-wife disentangle from one another.

March 2022: Yes, you CAN sit with us, because EVERYone is welcome at *Buffy* Prom! (Especially when it's happening at Torrance High School, a.k.a. Sunnydale High!)

March 2022: The Torrance High courtyard (instantly recognizable to those who watched *Buffy* Seasons 1–3) dressed and lit for *Buffy* Prom. Jake West

March 2022: It was a very good year. Jake West

March 2022: Jenny's Lestat-inspired getup finally makes it out of the closet and onto the dance floor. Jake West

September 2022: Two podcasters frantically communicating about a detail we can no longer recall as we prepare for night one of our *Buffering* finale weekend at The Bell House. Krista Schlueter

September 2022: Ready to take the stage and sing many *Buffering* songs together! (If you let her, Jenny would wear this tailcoat to literally every occasion.) Krista Schlueter

September 2022: Singing "The End of the Episode" to our beloved Scoobies to close out night 2 of our finale weekend. Krista Schlueter

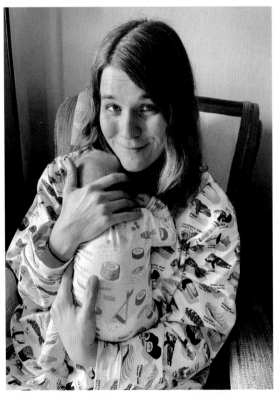

September 2022: The final howl-out with so many of the amazing people who helped make *Buffering* what it was and is. L-R: Mackenzie MacDade, Emily McLongstreet, Jeremy Rodriguez, Alba Daza, LaToya Ferguson, Morgan Lutich, Jenny Owen Youngs, Kristin Russo, and Joanna Robinson. Krista Schlueter

December 2022: Jenny and a potato-sized Alderic wearing the well-traveled and infinitely-loved Traveling Yummy Sushi Pajamas

OPPOSITE PAGE:

Some more of *Buffering's* tiniest Scoobies across the globe in the Traveling Yummy Sushi Pajamas (still in rotation!)

FOUR
WEEKS

IF THE
APOCALYPSE
COMES
BEEP ME

The mantis mask throughout the years, culminating in our Mantis Army on fina night and a retired (at least temporarily) mask after years of service. Molly Adams, Krista Schlueter, and Savannah Lauren.

chapter five

THE WEIGHT OF
THE WORLD

A wise man once said the years start coming and they don't stop coming, and this universal truth has perhaps never been *quite* so true as it is for Buffy Summers in Season 5. In order to make certain the audience knows the stakes (pun intended) have never been higher, the show kicks things off by pitting our intrepid Slayer against the vampire of all vampires: frigging *Dracula*. Vlad, as in the Impaler. The Prince of Darkness himself! Shortly after Buffy sends the Count packing, along with his luggage trunks, sexy succubi, and crates of special dirt, another new Sunnydale arrival appears: Buffy's kid sister, Dawn.

Did Buffy have a sister in the previous four seasons of this television show? Depends on whom you ask! Dawn is new to the series, but not new to the universe. She began her existence as a concentration of energy, a mystical key that a dark god named Glory wants to use to open a pathway to her home dimension. Alas, such an opening would mean the end of Earth as we know it, so a brotherhood of anti-Glory monks entered the key into a sort of witness protection program, re-forming it into a sister-shaped human being and inserting her into the Summers home. The monks thoughtfully constructed false memories for Buffy, her mom, all of the Scoobies, and everyone Dawn would have any reason to know; nobody bats an eye when she enters the show as though she'd always been there (with the extreme exception of every viewer, who we imagine all screamed, "What the *fuck*?!" in outraged unison across the globe when the episode originally aired).[1]

Now, in addition to Joyce, a mother she loves dearly, Buffy has another family member whom she will protect at all costs. However, there is a lesson Buffy has yet to learn: she cannot protect everyone from everything, and though her strength and skills are formidable when it comes to combating supernatural dangers, she has no inherent advantage when facing the mundane threats of the ordinary world. A vampire Slayer has no special powers against the natural failings of a deteriorating human body, and just after gaining a sister, Buffy loses her mother. The weight that rests on her shoulders compounds exponentially as she becomes the head of her household and the guardian of her young sister, all while continuing to stand as the last line of defense against the forces of darkness, which are suddenly darker than ever.

---

1 A delightful and long-running tradition in the *Buffy* community is to prank new viewers when they get to this point in the series. If a newbie screams in disbelief, "Buffy has a *sister*?!" the seasoned viewer will deadpan, shrug, and say something along the lines of, "Yeah, her name is Dawn! You don't remember her? She's been here the whole time!"

No prophecy
Could undo what has to be
You and me

Kristin

We took a whopping five months off between the end of Season 4 and the start of Season 5—the longest break we'd ever taken from podcasting with each other. We needed time and space, and our listeners had let us know in no uncertain terms that they wanted us to take care of ourselves first and that they would be there when we returned. (Bless them.) Jenny and I have always been people who desperately need that reminder.

While we did have some more time for ourselves during that break, getting anywhere close to a reasonable amount of time or space from each other was, as always, an impossibility. Season 4 ended in April 2019, and by the end of May I was back on a Los Angeles–bound plane to accomplish two business-related tasks: First, to go with Jenny to Stoopid Buddy Stoodios for a conversation with Seth Green, *Buffy*'s werewolf guitarist Oz and our biggest interview to date.[2] Then, the day after, to go with Jenny to our lawyer's offices so that we could

---

2 We'd been in touch with Seth's incredibly kind agent for *years* working toward this interview (Seth is a very busy guy!), and the 2019 release of *Changeland*—a film that he'd written and directed—provided the perfect press-adjacent opening for our conversation.

sign our official divorce paperwork. We were nothing if not true to form—a dash of *Buffy* and a pinch of personal drama.

Keeping even truer to form, when we left our lawyer's offices we decided to get a coffee together around the corner. Manicures after our divorce announcement, coffee after our divorce paperwork! They don't put these things in the handbook. When we sat down with our coffees, Jenny gasped. She leaned over and whispered, "James Van Der Beek is sitting outside." I have always told Jenny that she is somehow louder when she whispers than when she speaks normally, and this particular "whisper" did not come out quietly either. Luckily, James was none the wiser, and the legal end to our marriage was sealed with yet another golden thread of the 1990s weaving through our lives: Dawson himself on the day of our divorce.

Even in the moments in those months when we did have some space for ourselves, we both kept (far too) busy. I ran yet another queer sleepaway camp in Ojai, California (we queers will camp whenever and wherever you need us to); hosted my seventh annual All Ages Pride Party at Housing Works Bookstore in Manhattan; and started a whole new podcast called *The Boiler Room* with my beloved Joanna Robinson covering the nineteen precious episodes of my favorite show of all time: *My So-Called Life.* But as much as I pushed my body through time and space as though everything was *fine, actually*, my body had different opinions.

The day before I drove up from Los Angeles to Ojai to start camp that year, I had my first-ever ocular migraine. The location of this momentous event was none other than the dressing room of a Nordstrom Rack.

Since I have a history of anxiety and spent a few years plagued by panic attacks in my late twenties, I figured that when the light from the fluorescent bulbs above me started to wobble in my field of vision, I could just take a few deep breaths to steady myself (and the wobbly lights).

The more I practiced deep breathing, clutching a pair of white sneakers that I had reasoned might up my odds of finding someone to make out with me atop the queer mountain, the more the lights wobbled. By the time I had made my way up to the cash register, what appeared to be a crosshatched hologram of light had obscured my vision almost entirely.[3] I tried to joke about it with the cashier as I fumbled for my debit card, and as I left the store I saw (through the pinhole of vision I was afforded, and *with* my sneakers) a miracle: there was a LensCrafters *right next door*!

I bolted through the doors and all but assaulted the woman at the counter: "HI. I NEED TO SEE A DOCTOR RIGHT NOW. I CANNOT SEE ANYTHING." The very confused receptionist at first explained that I needed an appointment to see a doctor, at which point I burst into hysterical sobs and repeated the part about *not being able to see* just in case she'd missed that detail. She conceded and went to find the doctor.

Once I'd explained my imminent death to the doctor, she patiently told me that I could sit for another ten minutes or so with my eyes closed, and that if it was what she believed it to be—an ocular migraine—my vision would right itself. Then it was likely that I would have a whanging headache (those were not her professional doctor words, but was absolutely her meaning). She was correct, and though I have had a handful of other ocular migraines since, knowing what they are has meant that I do not think I am going blind and/or dying; I know how

---

3 Why did I go up to the cash register with sneakers when all of the store lights were dancing around my vision, you ask? Unclear.

to manage them, and I do not run into the nearest LensCrafters sob-demanding a doctor's attention.

I had seen a therapist for years, but had always been resistant to anxiety medication. Keeping on theme with my other Kristinisms, I always thought I could manage things on my own, without outside help. If I ate better, if I meditated, if I exercised more and drank less, I could find my center, and the lights (literally, metaphorically, etc.) would stop wobbling. Divorce played a much better hand than I did in many ways, and demanded, once and for all, that I ask for help. Later that summer, I saw a psychiatrist for the first time, and began taking an SSRI. My doctor prescribed a relatively low dose to start, and—once the drug had gotten into my system properly—I was amazed by how I felt. The change was subtle; I would get up to make dinner in moments where I previously could not have, I would go out to a movie with a friend when in the past I would have canceled. All of those small shifts, though, started to snowball and, for the first time in my life, the prospect of finding my center and holding on to it for measurable amounts of time seemed possible.

+ .+ . *.

Summer came to a close, and we were off to the *Buffering* races once again. We began our fifth season with werewolf interviews, freshly inked divorce papers, and a live taping of the season premiere—"Buffy vs. Dracula"—in Philadelphia. The event date: *Friday the thirteenth*!!

An auspicious day for hundreds of *Buffy* fans to gather and celebrate the meeting of the infamous Dracula and our titular

Slayer, indeed. The event was held at World Cafe Live, and it launched our fifth season more epically than we'd ever launched a season prior. World Cafe Live went absolutely *ham* on a custom menu including dishes like "Once More, with Chicken" and "We Attack the Mayor with Hummus," and cocktails such as "Band Candy" (dark rum, Campari, pineapple, passionfruit, lime) and "Gem of Amara" (rye whiskey, Amaro Averna, orange bitters), and by now our listeners knew the drill and had prepared their cosplay costumes months in advance. Folks flew in from overseas. I wore red leather pants. Jenny wore her absolute favorite outfit of all time: anything she wanted but *with* a giant Dracula cape. Joanna Robinson flew out from Oakland to join us. We wore custom fangs.

Having fun, of course, didn't mean that things had gotten easier. While the first year of podcasting through our separation had run nearly entirely on some blend of grief, shock, and going through the motions, this second year posed an entirely new host of obstacles.

Had we been typical exes with typical lives, we probably would not have been speaking to each other much. Maybe, in a moment of weakness—in the middle of the night or after one too many drinks—we'd send a regretful text or go on Instagram to sleuth for updates. But we would not have been in a position to know, beat by beat, the personal details of each other's lives.

We were not typical, however. We were inextricably tied to each other *and* in an endless loop of seeing ourselves reflected in a *Buffy*verse mirror.

And Jenny was moving on.

When I first learned that Jenny was in a new relationship, I maintained hope that we would get back together. She had to move through this, I reasoned, and while the chasm had grown wider than I had imagined it could grow, she could—even across the span of three thousand miles—still find her way back to me and Sam. So despite having already fallen on my face again and again in that first year apart, I learned that there was still plenty left inside me that could break when Jenny told me that she and her new partner, Jess, would be moving in together.

We were only surviving our work lives by keeping our respective hearts on opposite sides of a very tall, very sturdy brick wall. We could laugh about things like Riley taking off Buffy's boot veeeery slowly and sexily as a method of foreplay; we could dig into deep wells of emotion when Buffy, Dawn, Giles, and the whole Scooby crew wrap Tara up in chosen family after her "magic" (read: queerness) makes her father and brother reject her; but we could only do those things if we did not have to think about what we meant, and did not mean, to each other.

As Jenny's relationship moved into new and more serious stages, that wall began to crumble. With any glimpse over to the other side, no matter how small, I found myself destroyed. Truly, deeply destroyed in a way that I had never known was possible. And no matter how diligently and desperately Jenny and I both picked up fallen bricks and jammed them back into the wall, we could not keep up.

But we kept showing up.

Buffy Prom was returning once more, and this time it would be hosted in early April at Brooklyn's Bell House. It was the right venue for us in many ways—it was a good size, it was in a great location, it was a very cool space—but it was also a complicated choice to make given the fact that (for all of those same reasons) it had been where we'd gotten married to each other. Could I podcast with Jenny over Zoom? Sure. Could

I podcast with Jenny in the same room together? Of course. Could I throw a live event and stand up in front of hundreds of people with Jenny on the same stage where, the last time we'd been there together, we'd *literally gotten married to each other*? I wasn't sure, but *maniacal laughter* *Why not try?*

When we made the decision to try this newest, wildest compartmentalization adventure, I never imagined that Jenny would want to bring Jess.

Foolish, foolish me.

Jess and I already knew each other from "the before times." We'd met for the first time when Jenny and I had gone to see Now, Now—Jess's band—play at Irving Plaza in 2012. Incredibly, this meeting aligned with my first-ever watch of *Buffy*, and also with Jess's first watch of it. What are the goddamn odds! She and I talked about all of our (very new) feelings about the show, and I had to cover my ears (literally saying "lalalala" loudly to protect myself from spoilers) while she discussed Spike and his soul with Jenny, as she was further along in her journey. Later, all three of us worked together when we brought Jess into the *Buffering*verse as the voice of Faith Lehane, singing on both "Faith, Hope & Trick" and "Bad Girls." We'd FaceTimed together—Jenny and I at our house in California and Jess at hers in Maine—to puzzle out lyrics, Jenny and Jess working out the musical shape of the songs. We'd had so much fun with those two songs that we'd crafted a bonus holiday track together as well, spoofing the problematic classic "Baby, It's Cold Outside" as a duet between Buffy and Faith. But since Jenny and I had separated, and since I had learned that she and Jess were in a partnership, Jess and I had not spoken.

When Jenny told me that she wanted to bring Jess to prom, it felt like the few muscles left keeping my body upright—

staggering already under the weight of it all—gave out. If Jess was there, how could I use my now well-oiled powers of compartmentalization to get the work done? In the little vacuum chamber that Jenny and I had crafted for ourselves, I could pretend away the loss of my marriage and the breaking of my heart and the presence of a new person who was making Jenny happy (in a way, my brain constantly screamed, that I could not). But I couldn't pretend it all away if the actual, tangible manifestation of our separation was in the room with me. *Buffy* Prom is not the kind of work you do tucked away in an office; there is no option to run to the bathroom and shut yourself in a stall for a nice, long cry before refilling your glass at the water cooler. Once Jenny and I are onstage, or gathered in a room with the *Buffering* crew, we are *on*. How could I possibly have the strength to do that lift—to be *on* at all!—without being able to protect myself from the reopening of wounds that had barely had enough time or space to heal?

I sent an email to both Jenny and Jess. I did my best to communicate my understanding of and respect for their partnership, to say that I understood that, as Jenny's partner, Jess would want to attend *Buffering* events and support Jenny and her work, and that I supported getting to that place. I also tried to explain that the work lift of *Buffy* Prom was a massive one; in addition to being there as my podcast-host self alongside Jenny, I also ran all of the event's logistics—I was the tour manager, so to speak, for all of our live events. For this prom in particular, we had a live taping planned for the night prior (our first-ever attempt at making prom a two-night affair) and two big recording sessions planned on the days before and after prom—four consecutive days of work that would, even under the best of circumstances, be a heavy lift. I also admitted that the emotional impact of being back in our wedding venue for the first time since our wedding was an unknown to me. Maybe it would be fine. Maybe it would not be. In the email, I said that it seemed "like a totally bananas time and place for us to first share space together," putting stress on all three of us in a way that did not seem in anyone's best interests. The note ended, "I'd sincerely appreciate it if this bridge was crossed in a slightly less intense way, at a slightly less intense time, in a slightly less intense place. I think that there's a better path than this one, and I'd advocate strongly for choosing it."

Jenny

When we wrapped up our fourth season, I decided to use our generous break to dedicate myself to as many non-*Buffering* endeavors as would fit. I filled my calendar with cowriting sessions. Many songs were made, but my favorite from this period was one that I wrote with Briston Maroney: "Cinnamon," a sweet little love song written from the perspective of being on tour and missing your partner, who's keeping the home fires burning. In July, I began recording an album with L.A. Exes[4]—a four-piece, Beatles- and Beach Boys–inspired surf-pop band I'd formed with a few friends. In August, I traveled to Bess Rogers's new home outside Nashville to continue working on the album we'd started back in 2018. She and her family had left Brooklyn and were now living on a farm alongside her parents and her aunt. A baby donkey had been born just eleven days before I arrived, and there were sheep and horses and chickens in residence as well. Whenever we needed to take a break from tracking vocals or guitars,

---

4 "No relation to Kristin."—Kristin

we'd head out to the fields to pet the new donkey foal or give the horses carrots.

That same month, I launched a new podcast with Helen Zaltzman called *Veronica Mars Investigations*. I was excited to branch out and try something new (developing chemistry with a new cohost) while still keeping one foot in an arena that felt reasonably familiar and comfortable (recapping the televised exploits of a petite blonde protagonist). I had met Helen at a podcast convention when Hrishikesh Hirway, the absolute king of getting his friends to be friends with each other, threw a very on-brand event in his hotel room (Cookie Party: Tim Tam Slam Edition).[5] I knew Helen from her fantastic language podcast *The Allusionist*, and though I was intimidated, I guess I managed to make a decent impression—decent enough that months later, when the *Veronica Mars* reboot was announced and Hrishi suggested we might enjoy recapping the series together, Helen agreed that it sounded like fun.

As always seems to be the case with summer vacation, though, it was over before I knew it, and Kristin and I dove back into *Buffy* in the fall. After an epic season launch in Philadelphia, we traveled to San Francisco for our last event of 2019, a live recording of "Fool for Love." Backstage before the event, Kristin checked her email and screamed.

"MARC BLUCAS SAID YES TO AN INTERVIEW!"

---

5 If you have never Tim Tam Slammed, allow me to explain the basic premise: A Tim Tam is a long, skinny Australian cookie composed of a chocolate coating wrapped around two crunchy biscuits and featuring a gooey chocolate center. In order to slam said Tim Tam, you must bite the ends off the cookie, creating a sort of cookie straw. Then you drink a hot beverage—say, tea—through the modified 'Tam, which melts down the innards of the cookie to a delicious molten ooze. YES.

I sat in a stunned, blissful silence.

Blucas played Riley Finn, Buffy's first real boyfriend after the implosion of her relationship with Angel. Riley was the polar opposite of her previous beau: all warm smiles instead of furrowed-brow brooding, shiny butterscotch locks in place of a dark spikey 'do, a Labradorian bounce in his step rather than deliberate, pantheresque padding. He was my favorite of all the *Buffy* hunks.

Kristin relayed the rest of the information as I sat, still frozen. "His agent says that if we could meet him in Los Angeles in two days, Marc could make it work." Kristin immediately changed her flights to accommodate. We certainly *could* meet up with Mr. Blucas, thank you very much.

Mathematically speaking, of all the time we spent discussing Riley on the podcast, at least 10 percent of our chatter was devoted to the size of Marc's hands, which are perfectly proportionate to his six-foot-two frame, but which were made to seem much larger due to how often they came into contact with Sarah Michelle Gellar, who was nearly a foot shorter. As a parting kindness after our interview, Marc graciously compared hand sizes with me, placing his palm against mine for a photograph that would go down in history[6] as one of the most important images ever captured. His hand was bigger, of course.

+.+.*.

The new year started off with quite a bang when I received an unexpected phone call from my dad one evening. Larry

---

6 My mind.

Youngs has watched *Jeopardy!* every night for my whole life, so when my phone started to buzz and his name displayed as the caller, I panicked. Wasn't *Jeopardy!* on right now?? Something had to be wrong. My stomach dropped and I braced myself as I answered the call. ". . . Hello?"

Something was, as it turned out, incredibly *right*! And cool! And amazing!! My dad was ringing to tell me that our podcast had been an answer on *Jeopardy! Jeopardy!*!!! ALEX TREBEC ASKED A QUESTION TO WHICH *WE* WERE THE ANSWER! I could barely keep from absolutely *exploding* as I hung up with my dad and immediately called Kristin. We were so beside ourselves with wonder and awe that we decided to print royal-blue T-shirts (to match the answer screens) with the prompt question emblazoned in white lettering (in *Jeopardy!* font) across the front, one for Larry Youngs himself and the rest for anyone who wanted to memorialize the occasion with us. We even included the typo from the answer slide, just as it appeared in the broadcast:

COMPLETES THE TITLE
OF A PODCAST
DEVOTED TO TO
A SARAH MICHELLE
GELLAR SERIES,
"BUFFERING . . ."

To this day, it is possible that nothing has made us feel as cool as *that* moment.

On the personal side, though, we were struggling with some of the shiny new facets of what it meant to coparent a podcast through a separation.

I was in a new relationship, and I was absolutely over the moon. I'd met Jess years earlier when her band Now, Now came through New York on tour with two other bands I was friends with, Jukebox the Ghost and Motion City Soundtrack. We had stayed in touch and eventually started dating, and things accelerated in a way neither of us saw coming. New love is exciting! New love is fun! New love is something nobody wants to discuss with their ex-wife!

Indeed, at this stage I would have preferred to keep the rest of my life completely separate from the podcast and from Kristin, but certain logistical and practical considerations made this impossible. We had a recording schedule to maintain, and songs that had to be written and produced. If I planned to go out of town for a few days to spend time with Jess, I had to add my "away" dates to our shared *Buffering* production calendar. Though it was my preference to keep the nature of my travel days to myself, Kristin would invariably have questions. Since she was our show's producer, she'd ask if I would be available for any work things that might arise or if I would be "off the grid." When I would tell her that I would not be able to take calls or answer questions during a given window, she would do her own math and conclude that I would be with Jess (admittedly, fairly easy math to do). Kristin was not happy that I was spending time with someone new, and I was not happy feeling like Kristin was keeping tabs on me. There were definitely better systems we could have put in place to protect our respective privacies, but for most of the life of the podcast, neither of us could draw a decent boundary between work and life, even before divorce or new partners got added to the mix.

It didn't help that we had spent years sharing everything.

As I flailed about, trying to make things feel normal, old reflexes would surface and bid me to tell Kristin about some funny thing that had happened. Those funny things often involved Jess, however. So in the middle of some business-related call, my mouth would start moving, then my brain would have to perform real-time, acrobatic edits to avoid mentioning details I knew would just lead to discomfort, weird silence, or tears. As much as I didn't want to upset my *ex*, even more than that I wanted to keep my *cohost* happy, and the pod wheels turning. I was all too aware that a distraught Kristin was not a collaborative Kristin. I loved our podcast, and I wanted very badly for our little weather-beaten, duct-taped-together ship to stay afloat.

As much as I wanted that, though, I also wanted the freedom to continue my new relationship, and to do so without feeling limited by my past marriage. I *needed* that, and I believed I deserved it. I wanted to take Jess to prom.

Our next *Buffy* Prom was scheduled for April 2020, over two years after Kristin and I had split. We lived in different cities, we led individual lives. I was involved with someone whom I deeply cared about, and although my brain understood that the situation was extremely complicated, my heart wanted what would have been, in 99.9 percent of similar circumstances, a very simple thing: to bring my partner to a work event.

Kristin, of course, did not see it this way.

We went around and around via email and text and conversation, and we were getting absolutely nowhere. Kristin could not imagine making this concession, and I could not imagine excluding my partner from another event—a night that was so important to me, that I put so much work into, that I wanted so much to share with her. I was stuck between a very hard rock and a very hard hard place, forcing the air from my lungs, crushing me a little more each day.

Both of Us

Fortunately, the universe would solve this prom stalemate for us. Unfortunately, it would do so with an experience unlike anything any of us, globally, had ever lived through.

A month before our sold-out *Buffy* Prom at The Bell House, the country went into pandemic lockdown. Prom was, of course, canceled. Instead, on the day our prom was supposed to have happened, we arranged a virtual gathering to watch *Buffy*'s "The Prom" episode in a big, weepy, confused pile of feelings. Jenny tuned in from Pasadena; Kristin watched from upstate New York, where she had accidentally wound up sheltering in place with her parents. The world felt unpredictable and *wrong*, yet through the uncertainty we could, once again, see little beacons shining. We squealed together when Angel walked into the prommified gymnasium to surprise Buffy, we laughed together at the ridiculous hellhound costuming, we cried together when Buffy was given her Class Protector award. Our listeners shared stories with us, telling us how they were taking care of each other, taking care of their neighbors, and coming up with ways to bring a little light into the current darkness. For the zillionth time, we found ourselves completely overwhelmed by the seemingly infinite energy of our community, whose members were always striving (not unlike a certain vampire Slayer we know and love) to make the world around them a better place, to keep each other safe even in the most dire of circumstances.

+ .+. .★.

That summer, George Floyd was murdered by the Minneapolis police. Protests ignited across the United States and, soon thereafter, around the globe. While we had always worked to dig deeper into the racially problematic parts of *Buffy* on the podcast, we were only able to do that work from our vantage point as two white women. On the one hand, we were just trying to have a good time and talk about a vampire show from the 1990s!! On the other (and notably much more important) hand, we were speaking to tens of thousands of folks across the globe each week, and with that came significant responsibility.

We talked to each other, we talked to friends, we cycled through dozens of ideas on how to properly take any step in any direction and do so responsibly, and all we knew after a week of spinning was that we didn't know. We needed more time to sit with it all, because simply continuing forward without taking the time to look at the foundations of our own work seemed like the wrong choice. Up to this point, we had recorded seventeen episodes of our fifth season, and—even though we had taken a five-month break between seasons—we took another six weeks off before returning.

When we came back, *Buffering* had taken a new shape.

We brought on two new team members. The first was Alba Daza, who had been a listener of ours since back in Season 2. During our time off, Alba had written to us about her experiences as an Afro-Latinx fan of both *Buffy* and *Buffering*. She shared what she loved about both, and also told us about the times she'd felt personally let down by things we'd missed in our coverage. Specifically, she noted how much she'd looked forward to hearing us discuss the extremely problematic elements surrounding the death of Forrest, one of the few recurring Black characters to appear in the series. She'd listened to our coverage, waiting for us to talk in depth about the moment in which Forrest is not only killed but gruesomely mutilated. While we'd talked about our sadness in losing Forrest, a character who'd been with us for the entire fourth season, we'd failed to discuss the problematic elements of his death. We'd brushed over it, missing the impact entirely. Alba told us how disappointed and lonely she'd felt as a result. She expressed a desire to help us in our work toward making the podcast a more actively antiracist space, and we were thrilled when she accepted our offer to come on board as a producer.

We also began an ongoing collaboration with Mackenzie MacDade, a Black, queer, neurodivergent activist with whom Kristin had worked numerous times as a consultant on antiracist work and who, as luck would have it, wrote her thesis about *Buffy*.

At the start of July, this new *Buffering* team returned to the work of making a podcast about *Buffy the Vampire Slayer*. With the growth of our team, our operating systems changed—in the first few seasons, our ears were the only ones that listened to the podcast before it went live, but now both Alba and Mack listened in and gave us their notes and feedback; Alba also watched the episodes of *Buffy* along with us during production and sent us notes or came into the conversation directly to add commentary; supplemental episodes were added to the docket to tackle issues that deserved more attention than they could get inside episodic discussions.

Together we approached the end of our fifth season. Somehow, *Buffering* had pressed on through a traumatizing presidential election, a miscarriage, a divorce, a political uprising, and a global pandemic. We hadn't known if we'd finish Season 3; we barely made it through Season 4; but now, nearing the end of Season 5, we had the resolve that can only be found when you've repeatedly walked through fire. We said to each other, again and again, that if we'd stayed standing through all of that, we could probably count on staying standing.

We closed the summer with our coverage of the Season 5 finale, "The Gift."

At this point in the series, Buffy has also managed to stay standing through a litany of disasters both personal and professional. Hell, the girl kicked things off by literally *dying* in the first season. She had to sacrifice the first person she'd ever fallen in love with; she watched her high school crumble to the ground on the very day of her graduation; she'd lost friends, classmates, and, very suddenly, her mom. It's hard to dream up something more challenging for her to endure, but the series rises to the occasion: in order for the world—and her sister—to survive, Buffy must give her own life. She does so, with no hesitation, gracefully.

She understands that the work has always been bigger than her.

THE GIFT

I gave what I had to give
I gave you my only gift
The easiest thing I ever did
Was let it go so you could live

No prophecy
Could undo what has to be
You and me
Built from our blood
All these memories
Without you then who would make more

I gave what I had to give
Became what the world needed
But the times before never felt quite like this
Let go of your hand so you could live

No prophecy
Could undo what has to be
You and me
Built from our blood
All these memories
I need you to stay and make more

You won't miss graduation
I won't have to miss my mom
Just let me do this thing
Let me move on

To close up the dark till it's gone
To close up the night before—

chapter six

ONCE MORE, WITH FEELING

When we last saw Buffy, she'd just made the ultimate sacrifice to save the world—and more importantly to save her sister, Dawn. Buffy died. For the second time. At the start of the sixth season, she is still six feet under the earth. The Scoobies have initiated a stopgap measure of deploying the Buffybot[1] to patrol Sunnydale, to keep the demons and vampires under the impression that this is still a world where they should be cautious; a world where the Chosen One is alive and well and ready to kick ass. Willow's grief, combined with her increasing magical ability, has led her to the world of dark magic. She locates a resurrection spell, ritually kills a cute little doe-eyed deer in the Sunnydale woods, then sits atop Buffy's grave with Xander, Anya, and Tara. Her eyes go black, and we all wait for Buffy to pop up from the soil with a Slayer quip on her lips so that we can forge ahead into a new year of slaying demons and having a blast while doing it.

---

1 A robot replica of the Slayer (the origin story of which is best saved for another time) programmed to fight and quip in equal measure, who is saving the Scoobies' butts right now.

But nothing happens. The earth keeps her. The Buffybot must continue to patrol. We must continue grieving.

A demon biker gang descends on the graveyard, and the Scoobies scatter into the night.

However, just when we are about to give up hope, a mystical miracle occurs as Buffy's desiccated corpse is refleshed and revived. We just had to wait! A ray of hope now shines down upon us; our heroine has been returned!

In the days that follow, we begin to learn the awful truth: Buffy—grave dirt caked beneath her nails, fingers bloodied from clawing out of her coffin and up through the earth, alone—is traumatized, disoriented, and devastated to be alive. She has no wisecracks for us.

She walks through a burning Sunnydale, lost.

I go the only way I've ever known:
A step, and then, again, another one

Kristin

In the earliest days of our relationship—before marriage, before moving to Los Angeles, before we even lived together in Brooklyn—Jenny and I spent countless mornings unlocking crossword puzzles together. We'd sit side by side in bed, drinking coffee with a copy of *The New York Times* in one of our laps, barely speaking as we passed a pencil back and forth between us. Crossword puzzles, for the uninitiated, really *are* puzzles—most of them rely less on knowing the answers to the clues given and more on using the surrounding words to unlock bigger and bigger pieces of the word puzzle. This kind of creative collaboration, paired with unlocking something together, was always at the root of our love for one another's company. It seemed that in every form our relationship would take, this would be how we'd bring out the best in each other.

Buffy's sixth season contains the episode "Once More, with Feeling," a full-on *musical* that features seventeen original songs and packs a *massive* narrative and emotional wallop.[2] As we prepared for its arrival in the *Buffering*verse, we wondered: How would we ever match this moment?

We already wove music into our episodic *Buffy* coverage, so it seemed reasonable to expand that musical scope in an attempt to pay tribute to one of the best-loved episodes within the fandom.

We started in a place that felt reasonable. Perhaps we could make more than one song for the episode—maybe two or three?

On our first day of planning, Jenny announced, "The most important thing for us to touch on, musically, is the levitating oral sex scene between Willow and Tara."

I agreed.[3]

---

2 These days, it's easy to take for granted that a show would make a musical episode, but at the time it was relatively novel in the television landscape!

3 By this point in the series, Willow and Tara are in a romantic relationship in full view of the other Scoobies and at-home audiences alike (about *time*, Standards and Practices!). This newfound visibility allows the forces of magic and *actual* sex to converge, yielding a scene in which Tara *sings a song* while Willow disappears off-screen to engage in some kind of *adult activity* during which they are *hovering above the bed. Magically.*

"Should we sing the introduction to the podcast, too, so listeners know: this is not a normal episode?"

"Oh. Yes. And I guess instead of singing from Buffy's point of view, we should be singing as ourselves? Two hosts trapped inside a musical podcast?!"

For the first time in years, there was a puzzle we were excited to solve together.

As we worked on writing that first song, we were having *fun*. We sat together on Zoom calls pondering the physics required for this never-before-seen act of floating copulation. Wouldn't it be hard to simultaneously maintain both the concentration required for levitating *and* enough focus to, er, get where you wanted to go in such an act? Also, were they *both* aloft in the air, and if so, would that make it hard to . . . hit your intended target? Do witches always have sex in midair?! As we pondered the myriad mysteries of mystical fornication, we found ourselves laughing together more than we had since before our divorce. We didn't know yet how big the thing we were creating would end up becoming, but we could feel its electricity as Jenny crafted chord progression after chord progression and we excitedly shifted around lyric ideas together in our shared Google Doc.

At this point, we had already established a long history of bringing our friends into the creative fold. Folks we'd known for years (decades, even) had joined us in seasons past—some voiced our favorite *Buffy* characters in song; others worked alongside Jenny to help compose, produce, and create the music; and many more brought their love for the show into our podcast conversations. No one had ever hesitated to join in on the *Buffering* fun when asked—and the musical episode was no exception.

Joanna Robinson, whom we honestly considered our third

cohost by this point, joined us on a song about Spike called "Problematic Fave," a number that dovetailed perfectly with one of our favorite recurrent Joanna themes: TV's classic bad boys who were up to no good but who were irresistible anyway.[4] Our newly instated consultant Mack and freshly minted producer Alba joined us as well, cowriting a song with Jenny to address their feelings about the character named Sweet.[5] Mack spoke to us early on in the season about her desire to address some of the more problematic aspects of having a Black character written by a predominantly white room of writers, so she and Alba took the lead on lyrics and the overall direction of the narrative, while Jenny focused on the chords and melody. LaToya Ferguson, who had recently taken over as the new host of *Angel on Top*, signed on to help us sing about what giant nerds we were[6]—and we managed to get twenty-eight of our listeners to contribute home-recorded vocals that appear on the final recording.

This musical—*our* musical—felt like a microcosm of *Buffering*'s big picture right from the jump: the more excited Jenny and I became about its creation, the more it grew, and the more people we brought into the fold, the more incredible (and hilarious and epic) it became. The sparks of joy that had started the podcast were flying once more; we were starting to feel like *us* again.

---

4 See *Game of Thrones*' Jaime Lannister, *Lost*'s Sawyer, and *My So-Called Life*'s Jordan Catalano.

5 Sweet is a demon summoned by Xander to bring "dances and songs" in the hope that his building relationship stress with Anya will dissipate, and that the music will ensure their marital bliss. The role of Sweet is played brilliantly by the late, great Hinton Battle.

6 LaToya is the biggest TV expert we know (possibly the biggest TV expert *ever*).

In the midst of the musical excitement, I celebrated my fortieth birthday. The pandemic had added a deeper sense of isolation to all of our lives, and for me this also meant making the decision to move from Brooklyn to upstate New York. While Brooklyn had offered me a familiar, comfortable, and much-needed landing pad in the wake of my divorce, I knew even at the time that my return to NYC was temporary. The pandemic accelerated my plans to move north in search of a little more space (and a little more greenery), and I was pleasantly surprised to find that I immediately felt at home in my new surroundings. My upstate apartment sat across the street from a small park, and in the warmer months many community organizations would use the public space to convene. I started volunteering with a local food collective that delivered meals to folks in need—a way to give back and to also get out of the house in a COVID-safe way—and learned about all of the different areas in my new city as I drove to the various homes, apartment complexes, and motels on my food drop-off lists. When I was home, I spent weeks on small home-improvement projects: I made wooden covers for the old radiators where my cats would curl up and sleep; I built a wall of small shelves in the bathroom for extra storage; I converted a large walk-in closet that sat off of the living room into a nearly soundproof recording room for podcasting (and, as it would turn out, for recording song vocals).

I am not a very extravagant birthday observer, but it was still a shock to realize that I would be hitting the milestone of forty at a time when I couldn't even safely gather with friends for a shared meal or cocktail. I've always loved the time I have alone, though, so as the December days ticked closer to the seventeenth, I started to get excited. My most treasured memories of life in NYC have always been the nights when I would take a favorite book out to dinner with me; I'd order an expensive glass of red wine and lose myself in the story, pause my reading to eat while eavesdropping on stilted first-date conversations, and, in the summer months, lean back and watch in wonder as hundreds of different lives passed by me in a city sidewalk blur. I started to plan a variation of this kind of night: I stocked up on fresh breads and pastries at the bakery; I bought a fancy bottle of Bordeaux at the local wine shop; I gathered all of the fixings for a charcuterie spread; I bought premade Manhattans from a nearby bar (thank you, pandemic, for popularizing to-go cocktails). And, in what felt like a birthday gift from the universe herself, a snowstorm was forecast for the very *day* of my birth!

I *love* snowstorms. Only a few days after we'd first moved to Los Angeles, one of NYC's biggest blizzards descended on the city; I was absolutely distraught to be so far away. An impending snowstorm brings a singular kind of quiet to a community, and a temporary state of solidarity—knowing nods in long grocery store lines signaling, "It's coming!! Let's get ready!" Four years after that missed blizzard, December 17, 2020, saw *seventeen inches* of snow blanket upstate New York. The peaceful silence and solitude of the storm, paired with some of my favorite food and drink, made for the best birthday I had ever had.

+ .+. ˙✳˙

At the start of the new year, Jenny and I moved into a new part of our work on the musical, which had now been given a name: *Once More with Once More, with Feeling*. Writing the songs was only one piece of the whole. As is usually the case with songs, they also had to be sung. As is *not* usually the case with songs, a very untrained singer in the form of *me* had to sing about 40 percent of the vocals. I had lived most of my life up until the making of this podcast musical thinking that once I had a few glasses of wine in me, I could belt along quite nicely with moderately talented singers such as Mariah Carey and Whitney Houston. Fortunately for most (and unfortunately for me), this was the first time I ever had to hear my vocals played back to me. Notably, alcohol consumption before singing did nothing to improve performance.

Thankfully Jenny was a wonderful teacher. She made an instructional video showing me the various vocal warm-ups she used before singing, and spent hours with me finding my best key for each song. She created multiple "scratch tracks" so that I could try singing on my own, or with her voice in my ear to help guide me; I learned that I did better on my own with melodies, but that when it came to harmonies, I had to mimic what Jenny had sung for me, note by note.

When we are podcasting or making other creative or business choices together, we tend to be fairly blunt in offering constructive criticism to one another—a product of being married to each other for years and also of having established a certain amount of foundational trust. This was different. Jenny was gentle and kind to me in ways that were reminiscent of other vulnerable points in my relationship with her; she understood that this was a scary new place for me to create, and seemed genuinely thrilled to be able to help. She was insistent that I could do a good job, and as I got the hang of things, she was incredibly affirming. It was an unconventional process, but as it went on, I got better. *We* got better.

Just like in our crossword puzzle years, we were unlocking the pieces together.

Jenny

Years before we began collaborating on a podcast musical as two barely reconciled ex-wives, we'd had a different experience of being brought back together by something dear to us. Three nights before Kristin left Los Angeles to move back to Brooklyn, Sam got very, very sick. Whether it was the result of constant exposure to the stress that poured off of us in waves at the time or eating some mystery item never intended to be ingested by cats, this was the kind of sickness that made her scrunch her whole body up in the farthest corner underneath the bed, entirely unreachable. Kristin called me in panicked tears, and I drove over immediately; together the three of us went to the twenty-four-hour emergency vet. As the minutes wore on into hours, I read aloud to Sam from a book about jungle cats that I found in the waiting room.

We'd adopted Sam at a very emotional time for us both, and we'd shaped so much of our life at home together around her little presence. We loved her without hesitation, and much of the sadness I felt about my marriage ending, and about Kristin leaving, was processed through my grief over this precious ball of floof being transplanted across the country, thousands of miles away from me.

When the doctors finally took Sam to the back to run diagnostic tests, it left Kristin and me sitting alone together in the waiting room. Here we were, in the middle of the night, both scared about losing a pet we loved dearly. In those moments waiting for Sam, my love for Kristin was uncomplicated. Loving something *with* someone makes it easier to see the love you have for each other.[7]

Ever since Kristin and Sam had arrived safely and settled into their new life in New York, our collaborative method had consisted of the at times nearly unthinkable act of simply putting one foot in front of the other. But as we started work on this musical installment of the podcast, the act of collaboration began to feel different: it was infused with an ease that had long been absent between us. I began looking forward to our time working together, instead of feeling the usual low hum of dread to which I'd grown accustomed. Our shared love of creating together was helping us rediscover each other; it had taken nearly three years, but we were starting to see glimmers of the things that made us enjoy one another's company back when we'd first met.

Our delight in the work resulted in a song output that neither of us expected. We wrote five new songs in *five weeks*. At a rate of one song per week, we both agreed that we should forge onward and write even more music for this special episode. After all, it was only September, and the episode wasn't due out until *February*.

While Kristin and I were working together to determine the concept, lyrics, and genre of each piece, I was the only one of us qualified to handle the rest of the lift. For the vast majority of our episodic recap songs, I sang all the vocals, played all

---

7 Rest easy, gentle reader, in the knowledge that Sam was okay—it appeared that she'd just gotten her tiny system as emotionally wrecked as ours were at the time, and after some rest and rehydration she was back to her old tricks of unspooling toilet paper rolls and climbing seemingly unclimbable structures once more.

the instruments, shaped the arrangements, and mixed the final recordings. For this massive new undertaking, I desperately needed musical support. Thank God, Hecate, and all other deities in earshot, because John Mark Nelson—a musician with whom I'd worked on many of my own projects—came on board to answer our prayers, adding instrumentation and production and ultimately mixing both the album of songs *and* the entire podcast.[8] I also reached out to an old tourmate of mine, Ben Thornewill of Jukebox the Ghost, and asked him to contribute his virtuosic piano skills to the project; every musical deserves some acrobatic keys!

Historically, we had a one-to-one ratio of original songs to episodes of *Buffy*—usually written from the perspective of Buffy and always sharing its title with the episode itself. This meant that in addition to songs about levitating lesbians and great big nerds, we would need to write a song called "Once More, with Feeling." Since the musical songs were from *our* perspective, but the episodic songs were from Buffy's, this song would have to pull double duty: it would have to be something Buffy could sing about her own experience, but also something that Kristin and I could sing from ours.

We had done this before for songs like "Prophecy Girl" (Buffy, fearing what would happen to her world if she could not keep fighting in the face of that season's Big Bad; us, fearing what would happen to ours if we could not keep fighting after the horrors of the 2016 presidential election), "Amends"

---

8 In addition to creating the songs, Kristin and I also worked to curate our standard podcast commentary *around* the music. Kristin drew a "map" of all the ins and outs for the various songs, and when we recorded the spoken part of the podcast, we also navigated the tricky process of hitting those marks (improvising everything in between, to keep it sounding podcasty!).

(Buffy singing to Angel to tell him that his life was worth living; us encouraging our many queer listeners whose isolation from family was magnified during the holiday season to "keep holding on"), and "Wild at Heart" (Willow singing to Oz about her broken heart as he left; many of our lyrics informed by Kristin's perspective as I ended our marriage).

Earlier in the sixth season, after the Scoobies have found and cleaned up the wandering, confused, and newly resurrected Buffy, and after both they and we realize that a shower and fresh clothes aren't enough to bring back any sense of normalcy, she reveals the truth to the unlikeliest of recipients: Spike. What she cannot tell her closest friends or her sister is that for the few months she spent under the ground, she felt peace—a peace she had not felt since becoming a Slayer. Death had given her the rest that the world could not, and then, just as she began to get used to that feeling, she woke up inside a coffin—*her own coffin*—and had to climb back up to keep fighting.

The traumatic events that ushered Buffy and her friends into the start of the season had left them feeling more alienated from each other than ever before; it seemed the only way they could find to tell each other the things that most needed saying was through song. Though it had come with its fair share of positive moments, we had been moving through an unpredictable emotional hellscape for the better part of three years; every time we felt we might be on solid ground, we would stumble again and question everything. The past few months of writing together had started to let more light into our working relationship, and that light had also helped us see each other more clearly—perhaps, we reasoned, this was a moment in the episode where Buffy could seek out the meaning in the dark, and also a moment where we could speak to that in our personal experience.

During our first writing session for the song, I reached around for a melody by singing nonsense syllables over the chord progression and asked Kristin what she thought. An earlier pass had felt a little too happy, and this melody was feeling closer to what we were both after—but Kristin had also heard actual words in what I'd just sung. "It sounded like you said 'playback,' and that made me think . . . it would be kind of beautiful if we were searching for music and we couldn't find it, and maybe we could find it in the playback." I replied with one of my usual "hmms," to let Kristin know that I was thinking, I was chewing, and we were moving forward. I sang the melody again, this time with the words, "Maybe we could find it in the playback," and then paused for a moment and started again. The words that came out next instantly became the refrain of the song:

I'm just trying to get some light back
Scared that it's forever gone
Maybe we can find it in the feedback
Somewhere there's a hidden song

It was what Buffy was reaching for and, of course, it was what we were reaching for too.

The story you most often hear about divorce, about heartbreak, is the story of an ending. A light switch flicked into the Off position. But what if you clicked the bulb back on? Perhaps the items in the room are now rearranged: the table scooted against the opposite wall, the couch flipped around, this painting hung three inches higher, that painting taken down and moved into storage or dropped off at Goodwill. Surely just because something is different to both of you now, that doesn't have to mean that it's no longer any good. It is still a room where things happened, and you don't need to lock the door and never return.

Buffy came back to a life that was painful, but still worth enduring pain for. We were finding our way back to a friendship that was not always easy to maintain, but that felt increasingly worth the maintenance.

Both of Us

Slowly but surely, song by song and layer by layer, our growing team began to build a catalog of what would become seventeen songs—one to match each of the seventeen songs in the original musical. We wrote a song about the mustard that the dry cleaner got out of a singing man's shirt. We wrote a song about how mad we were at Giles for making the confounding decision to leave his chosen daughter in one of her darkest hours. And we wrote a song about Xander and Anya's shared apprehension regarding their impending nuptials.

In the first act of the musical, Xander and Anya, who became engaged in the Season 5 finale, sing about their many (many, many) fears of committing to each other in the long-standing tradition known as holy matrimony (which was remarkably still an option for folks residing on the Hellmouth).

The song begins with fairly commonplace spousal (or soon-to-be spousal) complaints: Xander snores, Anya eats smelly cheeses, Xander doesn't do housework, Anya never says please, and on and on. As the song continues, though, they get to the heart of the matter. Anya doesn't want to tell

Xander that she is afraid he will betray her; Xander doesn't want to tell Anya that he fears he will never be enough for her.

Since this podcast musical of ours was us, Kristin and Jenny, singing about our thoughts on the episode and its music, we thought we'd tackle this one by singing *back* to Xander and Anya. We knew those fears well, and we also knew what unfolded when those fears became reality. Also, we reasoned, who better suited to give advice to two crazy kids afraid to get married than two crazy kids who seemed to be (against all odds!) finding new ways to connect to each other after a divorce?! We advised Xander and Anya that if they made promises that they ultimately found they couldn't keep, they always had the option of splitting up.

We called the song "You Can Always Get Divorced," and in it we encouraged them:

Take it from two girls who've been down the line
There's no knot so knotted it can't be untied

You can always get divorced
You might even be better friends if you reverse your course
You can always get divorced

If we weren't writing songs for a musical episode of our podcast, and if the narrative we were covering inside it did not involve two people very anxious about marrying one another, it's entirely possible that we would never have looked each other dead in the eye and considered aloud that getting divorced might in fact have been the best thing to ever happen to our relationship.

+ .+ .* :

Some of the most hilarious moments of this creative process happened as we got closer to the finish line. Kristin got accidentally drunk on a bottle of Sancerre and bing-bonged her way through a take of "You Can Always Get Divorced" during which she forgot all of the actual lyrics and instead improvised with her own. The track made Joanna Robinson laugh so hard for so many days that we released it publicly as a little treat. Jenny made a last-minute decision to add what she emphatically referred to as a "choir of villagers" to our song about levitatilingus. With no warning, she texted Kristin and John Mark that she'd uploaded twenty new vocal tracks (*twenty!!*) to the session folder, each of them sung by Jenny but differentiated by a regional accent (Medieval Villager! Long Island Villager! Southern Fried Villager!). Each villager cried out in glorious harmony that they, the people of this fictitious (but very demanding) village, had a *right* to know exactly how the act of levitatilingus was executed.

Time moves strangely when you're making a podcast musical, and after what felt like ten years (but also ten minutes), we were at last (but also suddenly) within spitting distance of finishing our Herculean labors. In the eleventh hour we realized, later than anyone would have liked, that to really make our project feel complete, we needed to add that most vital of musical theater traditions: an overture. An overture serves as an instrumental introduction, taking pieces of different songs from throughout the musical and artfully stitching them together to create a sort of seamless sonic tapestry that primes the audience for that which is to come. We sent up a flare to our house pianist Ben Thornewill mere days before our final deadline, and he did not disappoint. On January 29, we sent Ben the four songs that we wanted to include, and on January 31 he sent us a gorgeous piano recording that wove fragments from all the songs together and led into the opening number, "Hello and Welcome," perfectly. John Mark artfully added instrumentation to support the piano, using timpani, crash cymbals, penny whistle, strings, and more, essentially becoming our one-man pit orchestra.

"Overture / Hello and Welcome" would be the first track our listeners would experience, but it was the last song to be completed. We spent a lot of time in our cars back in 2020—in many ways, they'd become an extra room in our homes that could move about to different locations—and Kristin had taken herself "out to coffee" on the day she first listened. This meant she'd driven to the nearby coffeeshop, masked, purchased a to-go coffee, returned to her car and sanitized both the cup *and* her hands, and then parked her car so that she could look out at some local trees while she sipped her beverage. When she pressed Play and the first notes from Ben's overture hit her ears, she wept. Jenny was more experienced at creating a recorded body of musical work and then listening to the finished product; she was able to hold on until the timpani roll at the end of the final song, "Codawooooooooo" (the title was a mashup of "coda," the word for a concluding passage of a piece of music, and our weekly pod signoff, "And 'til next time, awoooooooo!"), before she, too, sobbed.

It was finished.

We'd sat together for hours (and hours and hours) doing this *thing* we loved doing: creating work together that we found beautiful, that we found joy in, that brought us a deep sense of satisfaction. We had returned to a space that we'd only ever occupied as two people in love and had flipped the light switch back on, terrified of finding that the other person we had loved so fiercely would no longer be there. Instead we had found that the best parts of us were even more powerful after the dark had gone.

ONCE MORE, WITH FEELING

I'm just trying to get some light back
Scared that it's forever gone
Maybe we can find it in the feedback
Somewhere there's a hidden song

I go the only way I've ever known:
A step, and then, again, another one

I'm just trying to get some light back
Scared that it's forever gone
Maybe we can find it in the feedback
Somewhere there's a hidden song

I fight the only way I've ever done:
A step, and then, again, another one

I'm just trying to get some light back
Scared that it's forever gone
Maybe we can find it in the feedback
Somewhere there's a hidden song

chapter seven

SLAYERS, EVERY ONE OF US

At first glance, *Buffy* is a story about the Chosen One, but it very quickly reveals itself to be a story about the Chosen One and her friends. Buffy is able to triumph again and again because of the support and love of her companions, allowing her to far outlast the typical life expectancy of a Slayer. Even the grave is no match for this squad; Buffy is brought back to life not once but *twice* by the people who love her.

In the show's final season, our heroine has just started to get the hang of being a guardian to Dawn when a new threat drives a whole host of pseudo-siblings to the Summers house. The First Evil is working to end the Slayer line, tracking down and killing every girl in the world who *could* be the next Chosen One. These girls fittingly come to be known as Potentials. Many are slain by agents of the First, but those who survive find asylum at Buffy's house. The floors are gradually overtaken by the Potentials' sleeping bags, and the Scoobies also begin bunking at command central. (We've only ever seen one bathroom in the house; hopefully there are more.) The young newcomers are educated, trained, and battle tested while the more seasoned Scoobies work with increasing desperation to find any possible weakness in their new foe.

The battles we see at the beginning of the season are brutal; Buffy and the Potentials are hurled through walls, against floors, and into all manner of very hard objects as they come up against the seemingly limitless power of their enemy. We rarely see Buffy with lasting cuts or bruises—accelerated healing is one of the occupational perks of Slayerhood—but the wounds she suffers this season linger uncomfortably. She is exhausted, and for once she *looks* exhausted. This time, the residents of Sunnydale are fleeing—something that has never happened before. We've seen other apocalypses hit this town, but this one is different.

Nothing is as it once was; everything feels unfamiliar and on the brink of destruction. By the end of the series, Buffy and her friends have lost many loved ones, and Sunnydale has been entirely swallowed by the Hellmouth.

Came to this town
And I looked all around
Thought that I was alone
But I never was

Both of Us

By September 2021, we were wrapping up the sixth season of *Buffering the Vampire Slayer* with the overwhelming realization that we had, somehow, arrived at the beginning of the end.

After many moments spent fearing that we'd break under the weight of our own lives before we could finish talking about Buffy trying not to break under the weight of hers, we'd gotten far enough to know that there was now no turning back. We would finish the entire series and, incredibly, we would do it together.

With those feelings of epic achievement coursing through our veins, we made some very big decisions. The first of those decisions was to bring back our long-lost *Buffy* Prom that coming March and host it at—wait for it!!—Sunnydale High School. *The* Sunnydale High School.

The first three seasons of *Buffy* take place during Buffy's sophomore, junior, and senior years at Sunnydale High. Much of those first three seasons was filmed at Torrance High School in California—a high school that had served as a filming location for many shows and movies in the 1990s.[1]

When we'd first started the podcast, back when we still lived in Southern California, we'd driven down to Torrance High School with a pie-in-the-sky dream of one day doing some kind of event on the grounds. We were shocked (and thrilled!) to learn that Chris Johnson, the man in charge of the high school's event programming and space rentals, was *the very same guy* who'd managed the location back when *Buffy* was filming. On that initial visit we'd taken photos and gathered event-specific information. We also lost our minds upon seeing the courtyard with *Buffy*'s infamous fountain, framed by the outdoor hallways that she'd walked through with Willow, Xander, and Cordelia, and the tall stone staircase with the railing that she'd once sprinted up to use as a springboard into the

---

1 Including *Beverly Hills, 90210* and *She's All That*—featuring a cameo from Sarah Michelle Gellar and starring her future husband, Freddie Prinze, Jr.!

school's bell tower while defusing a violently upset classmate in time to both save him and preserve the safety of the other students. There, in front of our eyes, was the real thing, the actual physical place where the Scoobies had met for the first time, where they'd decorated the insides of their lockers, and where they'd courageously smote various vampires, demons, and poltergeists.

We kept in touch with Chris over the years and had a few "almosts" when it came to organizing an event at Torrance High, but it had never been the right time . . . until *now*! What better time to make it work than our final season? And what better use of the Torrance courtyard—a.k.a. the Sunnydale courtyard—than as *Buffy* Prom central?!

On Halloween, just three days before the premiere of our seventh and final season, we announced our plan, and tickets sold fast. Folks had already loved being able to gather together with fellow *Buffy* fans and dance to their favorite nineties music, but now they would have the chance to do that while feeling like they were inside the show itself.

One of the best parts of hosting a podcast about a thing that you love is that when your listeners are overcome with excitement, so are you. None of us could believe that it was really happening.

On March 12, 2022, promgoers would enter through the front of Torrance High School, which rivaled the courtyard for recognizable locations that played host to significant events throughout the show. There was the outdoor stairway where Xander rode his skateboard in the pilot episode of the series. There was the half-moon-shaped window where Angelus had killed Jenny Calendar. There was the grassy area to the right of the entrance where they'd sat in the wake of the Graduation Day Battle, looking out over a decimated Sunnydale High School. It was all there, and now folks decked out in prom attire and absolutely iconic cosplay would come through those same doors to dance, to sing, and to be with their *Buffering* family.

Up until this point in our personal journey, our most valuable survival tool had been compartmentalization. When we worked, we were *at work*. We did our best to keep discussions of dating, marriage, and anything tangentially related waaay off the table. Was it healthy? Probably not. Was it effective? Absolutely. The last time we were planning a prom, the pandemic freed us from having to sort out our office dating policy. This time there would be no escape!

But, hey, things were different now. Years had passed. Jenny was in fact *married* to Jess at this point. The wall *had* to come down. We all knew that Jess was coming to our Sunnydale prom, but—even though admittedly Kristin and Jess had been friendly with each other for years before our divorce was even a twinkle in our eyes—none of us really knew how to handle it.

Kristin

When Jenny emailed me about her engagement to Jess back in May 2020, I was sitting in my mom's car, just six weeks or so into pandemic lockdown, probably returning from a recent hunt for that most elusive of beasts: toilet paper.

Jenny's message said that she wanted me to hear the news from her before I learned it from the internet, which was kind. I am not sure that the same graces would have applied if we weren't actively working together, but we won't ever know

what that path would have had in store for either of us. She also
wrote that she hoped I would be happy for her. In May 2020, I
was not. I thanked her for letting me know and I asked that she
give me two days' padding between the public announcement
of her engagement and our next podcast recording. Incredibly,
the two episodes that we were sandwiched between at the time
were "The Body" and "Forever"—also known as two of the
absolute saddest episodes of the show: the one where Buffy's
mom dies, and the one where the Scoobies bury her.

Ouch.

We kept working. We also kept trying to do the impossible:
confine life to one side of the wall and work to the other. A little less than a year later, Jenny called to tell me that she and Jess
had gotten married in a small backyard ceremony in Maine.

That time, I received the news while sitting on the couch
in my house—I'd purchased my very own *house!*—in upstate
New York. In the eleven months that had passed since Jenny's
engagement email, I had started to see flickers of what my life
could look like as my heart found itself healing. So when Jenny
told me this news, I found I *was* happy for her. I was happy for
both of them. I told Jenny that I loved her, and—now that I
could see past the pain of it all (even if just in flickers!)—loving
her meant that her happiness made me happy, too.

A few months later, Jenny and I were on a call discussing
our biggest *Buffy* Prom to date: to mark *Buffy's* twenty-fifth
anniversary, we'd be flying out to California to host prom at
Torrance High School. It would be the first time that Jess and
I had been in the same space together since the divorce, and it
was also the first time that I could, without my knees knock-
ing together and my heart dropping down into my stomach,
imagine being in a space with both her and Jenny (and a few
hundred of our closest friends). As the conversation wound to

a close, I told Jenny that I had been thinking on an idea for the past few weeks and wanted to get her feedback. "When we play 'Kiss from a Rose' and the *Buffering* production team comes up to sing with us, I thought it would be nice if Jess came up to sing with us, too."

Jenny was quiet; a long, thoughtful Jenny-pause. Then she cried.

"Yes. That would be really nice."

The next day, Jess and I opened up a text exchange that led to a FaceTime, just the two of us (no Jennys allowed!). We were both incredibly nervous when the call began, but we are both forthright people, so we were honest about the terror we'd felt leading up to this moment, and then got right into it.

Four years is a long time to have existed on opposite sides of a wall, and we talked about some of the ways that the separation had done a disservice to both of us, to Jenny, and to all of our overall relationships. We each apologized for things we wished we'd done better. We laughed about moments we'd not previously gotten to share with each other, like Jess's ongoing experience of her car's speaker connecting to Jenny's phone while I was on the line—"I would just sit frozen in panic and be very quiet until it disconnected!" We talked about being in partnership with Jenny, and began what would become an ongoing, synchronized eyeroll at many of the things we pretended to hate but secretly loved about the Labrador Retriever that is Jennifer Youngs. Surprising no one, we had a good deal in common with each other.

When I arrived in Torrance, Jenny and Jess both came down to meet me in the parking lot of our hotel. Nerves had returned (this was no longer a virtual meeting, this was the *real thing!*), but I figured that *surely* we could say our hellos and commence a new era of working together, side by side, all wives and ex-wives allowed.

I leaned forward and pulled Jess in. We embraced, then attempted to do the thing that most folks do after embracing: step back and continue the pleasantries. However, we couldn't pull apart. Unbeknownst to us both, my hoop earring had caught the ear band of Jess's mask in our embrace and, no matter how we moved our heads around, we could not seem to disentangle. Jenny, who could see what had happened, was laughing too hard to help us apart, though she had absolutely no problem taking dozens of photos of the scenario from multiple angles. After the photo shoot, Jenny unhooked my earring from Jess's mask and, voila, the ice was broken.

Prom itself was magical.

We gathered in the school theater the night before the dance to talk about the most epic moments from Buffy's high school years. I had commissioned custom letterman jackets for both Jenny and myself, in the Sunnydale colors of maroon and gold and with a big felted S on the front. Jenny wore hers as she entered from the back of the auditorium, running all the way up the aisle as the crowd cheered her on from their seats and while I waited for her (laughing hysterically) from center stage. We talked to some of our favorite people—Joanna Robinson, LaToya Ferguson, and Morgan Lutich among them—about their favorite *Buffy* moments set inside Sunnydale High. We reminisced about the time that the mayor of Sunnydale met up with the Scoobies in the cafeteria ("right over there!" we exclaimed, pointing to the building next to the auditorium, where the scene had been shot) to retrieve his box of magical spiders and *also* to tell Angel and Buffy that their love could never last (rude!); we laughed about the time that Xander, Willow, and Buffy chaotically tried to perform a scene from *Oedipus Rex* in front of a full high school auditorium to distract from the murderous demon they'd just defeated ("right *here*," we yelled, although actually that scene was filmed in some other auditorium); and we sat in our feelings discussing the time that the spirits of two ill-fated lovers from the 1950s who'd died inside the high school possessed the bodies of Buffy and a then-evil Angelus, giving us a kiss that we'd longed for since Angel had lost his soul several episodes prior.

The following night, we prommed harder than we'd ever prommed. Jenny lost her mind doing the Macarena with hundreds of *Buffy* fans (later, folks looked back on this moment and said they'd felt like they'd been "in some kind of trance," and they thought it would never end "but in a good way," and also "is the Macarena usually that long?"); we blew up massive gold mylar balloons that spelled out Faith's classic catchphrase "5 X 5"; we served nineties-themed snacks including Gushers, Smartfood Popcorn, Fruit Roll-Ups, and an assortment of Capri Sun juice packs; and we sang "Kiss from a Rose" with Jess, Jenny, and me all standing together on the balcony with the rest of the folks who'd worked with us to make *Buffering*.

I'd brought a date with me that year too, and she and Jess wore our Sunnydale letterman jackets around the campus, conspiring on after-prom party plans and how they'd convince us both to drive them to In-N-Out on the way home.

Toward the end of the night (and before that hard-earned trip to In-N-Out), some of our listeners asked if we'd join them down in the courtyard. When we arrived, they encircled us and handed us each a large handmade golden key adorned with a serpent head and a capital B in the *Buffy* title font instantly recognizable to any fan. A few of them stepped forward out of the group, mics in hand, and read to us:

Twenty-five years ago, Buffy Summers was called to be the one to stand against the vampires, the demons, and the forces of darkness—one girl in all the world. Not quite so long ago, two other girls in the world chose all of us, and so many more, as their chosen family—and now here we are—at Sunnydale High.

Standing here to thank you, Kristin and Jenny, at Sunnydale High School is surreal.

Seeing our friends that we've made our family after two years apart feels like coming home. I don't think anyone could have predicted what this community would become to so many of us when we first began listening, or that the connection we feel to *Buffering* would grow to rival our connection to *Buffy* itself.

We've grown as a community, we've grown as people. We've supported each other through our success, milestones, joy, and hardship.

We've watched our friends grow and change as the community grew and changed. While we may not all know each other now like we did in the beginning, we have each other and hold each other like a real family.

Buffering, like *Buffy*, has taught us what it means to be "Chosen." Standing here on this hallowed hellmouth, we thank you, Kristin and Jenny, for giving us our Chosen family—and for bringing us together again after years apart.

May these dimension-opening keys only take you to beautiful places.[2]

---

2 Thank you to our Scoobies Morgan Gray and Liv Mammone for writing these incredibly beautiful words, and Rachael Hayes for handcrafting our stunning dimension-opening keys.

Jenny

Of the many reasons that my soul was fractured when we had to cancel our 2020 prom, high among them was the fact that the cancellation left my prom outfit hanging in the closet for two long years. Kristin and I had decided at the time that rather than go with traditional modern formal wear as we had in years past, we would instead lean into something from the *Interview with the Vampire* lookbook. Thus I had spent hours piecing together an outfit that felt appropriately Victorian, and appropriately dramatic, from websites like draculaclothing.com and historicalemporium.com: a scarlet tailcoat embroidered with metallic golden thread, a replica of a nineteenth-century officer's vest, a high-collar shirt with sleeves poofy enough to make Mr. Darcy jealous, and of course, without a doubt the most vital of garments for this ensemble, a cravat. This majestic assemblage of attire had been languishing, awaiting its moment, and now finally that moment drew nigh!

While those two years were not eventful for my Lestat-inspired getup, the shape of my life had changed immensely. Jess and I had welcomed a puppy into our home in Pasadena; Frank was a Boston terrier full of boundless enthusiasm who quickly became the center of the household. Not long after this furry little tornado of joy became part of the family, I asked Jess to go for a drive with me up the Angeles Crest Highway on the pretense that it would be nice to get out of the house. We drove farther and farther up through the mountains until we reached an overlook that felt appropriately stunning for what I had in mind. When we got out of the car, I asked Jess to marry me. She said yes. We laughed and hugged and beamed at one another, and Frank rolled celebratorily back and forth on the ground, coating himself in Southern California dust.

Some months later, as Jess, young Frank, and I sat on the couch watching television, a most curious thing happened: the living room began to heave and sway, which at the very least seemed like highly inappropriate behavior for a room. It felt as though the house was no longer a building with a foundation but rather a boat on a churning sea, and this went on for what felt like a weird eternity. When the biggest earthquake I had ever experienced finally passed and the world found its way back to stillness, Jess and I looked at each other and agreed that it was well past time for us to get the hell out of Los Angeles. We immediately began hatching a plan for our migration to a quiet coastal area of Maine where Jess grew up—a town we'd always planned to move to *eventually* . . . never expecting that "eventually" would arrive quite so soon. Once settled in our new home, and with no desire to wait, Jess and I were married in our yard, under a sky full of stars, with a handful of friends looking on. Frank, already blessed with the natural tuxedo coloring of his breed, wore a tie.

While Frank—despite his God-given formal wear—was not able to attend prom, I was immensely happy to head into this momentous weekend with Jess by my side.

+ .+. .+.

Earlier in the season, we'd written a Sunnydale alma mater for "Lessons," the first episode of the season, in which Dawn starts her freshman year at the newly rebuilt Sunnydale High School. The song was an ode to the Sunnydale High that came before, and at prom we donned maroon graduation caps with gold tassels as a crowd of six hundred Scoobies, gathered in the Torrance High auditorium, sang along with us:

> *From the local zoo hyena pit to the peak of Kingman's Bluff*
> *We may not live to graduate but at least you've raised us tough*
> *You've taught us life's worst lesson: it's hard to stay alive*
> *Sunnydale, oh Sunnydale, only the strong survive*

Looking out into the audience as we all joined our voices together for one song from a songbook that would eventually total 160, I felt a weight on my heart, reminding me that while we weren't quite finished yet, the end was in sight.

In July, after a long period of recovery from Macarena-ing our way through *Buffy* Prom, we made our way to Chicago to celebrate the return of our favorite leather-clad Bostonian Slayer. Faith returns to Sunnydale in the episode "Dirty Girls," and we hosted a two-night "Dirty Girls Weekend" (insert eyeballs emoji here) in her honor with a night of music and Faith appreciation followed by a live taping at Lincoln Hall.

We'd hatched this wild idea back in Torrance, at *Buffy* Prom, where Jess, Kristin, and I hung out for the first time in years. Buzzing with prom energy (and also probably some whiskey energy), we came to a realization: After a long absence, Faith returns to the *Buffy*verse in the seventh season of the show—which meant that the voice of Faith could also return to *our* show. *Jess was that voice.* It was time for Jess to rejoin the *Buffering*verse!

Of course, as the old saying goes, with great wife-and-ex-wife integration comes great apprehension. We all had a great time together at prom, but what if that was a fluke?

In an effort to leave little downtime for awkward silences or general weirdness to arise, we filled the gaps in our Chicago itinerary with as much activity as possible. We felt it was vital to indulge in a local specialty and ordered deep-dish pizza from the two most recommended purveyors in town, performing a taste test to determine which one was best (the consensus: Pequod's). We also wound up at a beer garden serving—if you can believe it, and I hope you can—a hefeweizen infused with the *Ghostbusters* Hi-C flavor Ecto Cooler. Famously afraid of absolutely no ghosts, I drank and enjoyed.

All in all, the weekend went off without a hitch. Jess and I performed every duet that we'd written from the perspective of the two Slayers, including the brand-new song for "Dirty Girls." I also introduced Kristin to a divisive liqueur first distilled—and still made today—in Chicago. Jeppson's Malört is the kind of beverage best sprung on someone with an unsuspecting palate (tasting notes range from "grapefruit rind" to "gasoline") in view of their friends, so I got Kristin to try her first shot of Malört onstage in front of everyone (major "Malört face" documented by all).

One of my favorite moments of the weekend was when the three of us performed "Buffy, It's Cold Outside." Back in 2017, when Faith had first arrived on the scene of the pod, Kristin and I had rewritten the lyrics to this notoriously problematic Christmas classic to be an exchange between Buffy and Faith. Jess had sung the Faith to my Buffy, with lyrics that focused on subject matter such as the deliciousness of Buffy's nog and how, given that the hands of vampires were surely quite cold, Buffy should consider alternative options. For reasons that are likely obvious, after the Christmas of 2017, we did not promote the song much. Now, at long last, we could bring our holiday masterpiece back to the masses.

In anticipation of this momentous occasion, Kristin had purchased scarves for all three of us and a giant bag of fake snow. Jess and I would sing, and Kristin would participate by scattering snow around us—a Christmas in July, divorce-to-remarriage miracle!

However, during soundcheck that day, the gentleman running sound explained to us that we couldn't use the powdered snow onstage—the venue had a strict policy that dictated no confetti or other small materials could be used without a hefty cleanup fee. For reasons that went far past this "no snow allowed" revelation, Kristin was crushed. Crushed to the point where, though our friend in the sound booth was none the wiser, I could tell that she was close to tears. In such a delicately tangled situation, the micro can become massive in an instant, and I knew it was important for Kristin to be a part of this song with Jess and me (and display her snow-as-comedy chops).

The gears of my brain immediately began to whirr. While Kristin ran some of our slides, I quietly excused myself from soundcheck and darted up to the green room in search of materials. Plain white paper was easy enough to source; I had a few extra sheets in my backpack, which I swiftly folded and refolded until they became many-layered triangles. I didn't have any scissors, but the venue manager was kind enough to loan me some. I engaged in some swift, deliberate snipping. Then I popped back down to the stage to ask Kristin if she'd happened to bring any dental floss with her. Though Kristin looked at me like I had sprouted two additional heads, she answered in the affirmative and told me where I could find it. I took the stairs two at a time back up to the green room to finish my impromptu arts and crafts project. A few knots and a handful of minutes later, I returned to the stage once more and, beaming, bestowed unto Kristin the fruits of my labors: two handmade paper snowflakes, the stuff that elementary school classroom bulletin board dreams are made of, dangling from long strands of dental floss, which would allow Kristin to "make it snow" behind me and Jess while we sang our festive duet. No cleaning fee need be incurred! The snow must go on!

Over the last decade and change, we had each learned a thing or two about how the other expressed love and care. Kristin's tendency, as you surely know at this point in the adventure, was simply to ascend the nearest mountain and profess her feelings loudly and with no hesitation, often more times than would ever be required. That was simply never my way. I tended more toward small, subtle gestures: gifting Kristin a small stone bear after a trip with my friends to Santa Fe; carefully packing a picnic basket with peanut butter and jelly sandwiches and ginger ale for a drive to the lake near my family home; leaving a small note on the kitchen counter before I would depart on tour. Kristin knew this about me, so was able to receive my gift in its fullest form. She could use words to let me know that she cared about me; I could make a snowflake.

Both of Us

Only four episodes remain in the series after "Dirty Girls." We had known for a long time that the finale of *Buffering* needed to be hosted in our forever-home city: New York. We had talked about going to The Bell House, and at the time we even knew we'd be writing a book together (this very book!). Kristin jokingly said, "Come on!!! The place we got *married* being the place we *end the whole journey*?!" Jenny, after telling Kristin for the millionth time that she used the word "journey" far too often, said we should also look at other options before we made the call.

So we did. We looked at St. Ann's Warehouse (no air conditioning) and we looked at Town Hall (too big) and at a gorgeous church that moonlighted as a performance venue (Them: Would we talk too explicitly about sex? Us: Almost certainly!). Then we looked at the Brooklyn Masonic Temple. It seemed perfect: it was the right size, it had air conditioning, and we got along well with the folks who worked in the space. We booked it. And then, just two months before the event, we got a call: water damage had been discovered in the basement of the space and they could not guarantee that it would be fixed in time for our event. Immediately, we called our friends at The Bell House. It seemed our storybook ending—wrapping up seven seasons of *Buffy* in the very same spot where we'd stood in 2013 to get married to each other—would happen after all.

After that initial call with The Bell House, we set the dates for our two-night finale.

On September 17, Jenny would play through a selection of our favorite *Buffering* songs and, for the first time ever, she'd play them with a full band.

On September 18, we would record our coverage of *Buffy*'s series finale, "Chosen," with a litany of special guests flying into New York to join us in conversation.

And then, though it seemed absolutely impossible, it would be over.

When we were still several months away from the finale, we each began experiencing physical reactions to our impending end. We would burst into tears at unexpected moments: in the middle of a taping, while pumping gasoline, in line at the grocery store. Our minds were consumed with the day-to-day tasks of recording episodes, planning finale details, and writing the songs that remained, but the mourning process had already begun in our bones.

+ ⸱+ ⸱*⸱

When we got to New York, we held a celebratory brunch for our main production staff along with some of our most integral Scooby contributors. Our wonderful Facebook moderators, Jeremy and Rosemary, were in for the event, as were "the two Emilys"—one whom we referred to as Brackets for her tireless work managing our Sexual Tension Award brackets,[3] and the other whom we'd nicknamed Back Patch for that one time she'd given us a gorgeous *Buffy* back patch (which now hangs in Kristin's office). Alex, who had run our UK-based store for years, came all the way from London to be with us. These were only some of the people who had made us, us. The people who had made *Buffering*.

We'd worked with our good friend and longtime collaborator Isabella Rotman to create custom drawings for this core crew of folks who'd worked with us over the years. In one of the most notable episodes of the series, "Hush," everyone in Sunnydale loses their voices as the terrifying demons known as the Gentlemen float through town cutting out the hearts of their victims. To plan their response, Buffy and crew gather together in an empty classroom where Giles draws out the battle plan on transparencies, which he places on an overhead projector one by one. The first transparency is a horribly (and hilariously) drawn Buffy holding (of all things) a bow and arrow. Giles writes across the top, "Buffy will patrol tonight."

---

3 Early in the series, we started running a listener poll for which we nominated four couplings (or throuplings) from each episode that we felt exhibited electric sexual tension. Our listeners voted to determine the episode's winners, and at the end of each season the episodic winners would all compete against one another in an epically sexy bracket. Winners for all seven seasons of the series can be found in Appendix E.

And so, Isabella handcrafted little horribly (and hilariously) drawn versions of each of us with our names across the top—"Alba will patrol tonight," "LaToya will patrol tonight," and so on. We framed each drawing and, at that brunch gathering, set them around the table before everyone arrived.

Our first night kicked off like something out of a dream: We huddled up side-stage with the band, talking and laughing and sipping whiskey while we waited for showtime to arrive. Of the 160 songs in *Buffering the Vampire Slayer*'s catalog, Jenny was able to narrow it down to her very favorite . . . 128 songs. From there, we had worked to somehow shave off 108 songs in order to get the setlist down to a manageable 20.

The moment the clock struck 8 P.M., a packed house of rowdy, ready-to-party *Buffering* enthusiasts could contain themselves no longer. A chant rose up from the crowd, unrelenting and quite loud, even backstage. *JEN-NY! JEN-NY! JEN-NY!* they thundered, offering Jenny a glimpse into what it might feel like to be Harry Styles. We hooted and guffawed, unable to fully get our brains around what was happening.

We'd decided to begin with "Hello and Welcome," the introductory duet of our musical episode, and to play the recording of the "Overture," which immediately precedes it, as our entrance music. This was meant to allow us time to get onstage, get our instruments, take a breath, and then start singing. The opening notes of the "Overture," though—since the moment we first heard them—have always taken our breath *away*. The song begins with a rapid piano arpeggio played repeatedly—invoking a palpable feeling of excitement about all that is to unfold. Then the music gradually slows and the gentle roll of a cymbal ushers in the first few recognizable notes of the musical. In that moment as we prepared to walk onto The Bell House stage, the music felt like it contained everything we'd created together since that very first recording in our Altadena home. It seemed our audience agreed: while they'd quieted momentarily as the lights dimmed and the music began, when we walked to center stage holding hands, a wall of enthusiastic screaming rose to meet us. It was the kind of screaming that could only be generated, we are convinced, by a room full of people united around a story they all love, coming to the end of a six-year journey of podcasts and live tapings and meetups, of building friendships and finding true loves, in this mini-universe we had somewhat accidentally created.

The night was an ecstatic blur as we bounced from bop to ballad and back again, with special guests popping up to join us. A custom THE BRONZE sign handcrafted by our listener Scout lit up the edge of the stage. We got to sing "You Can Always Get Divorced" together on the same stage where, nine years earlier, we had exchanged marriage vows. Kristin jokingly called out to her parents, who were in the audience, "I bet this isn't what you had in mind when I came out to you. . . ."

On the more tender side, Jenny dedicated the song "Enemies" to Kristin, as a nod to how far we had somehow managed to come since our separation four years earlier. In our musical take on the gutting end to the relationship between Buffy and Faith, we imagine Buffy shaking her head in disbelief and sorrow, wondering how she could feel so far away from someone with whom she has shared so much. By the end of the series, we—not unlike Buffy and Faith—had managed to swing all the way back around from a similarly low point to a place of deep friendship.

After choking up literally every single time she'd rehearsed the song prior to the show, Jenny was relieved to discover she was able to get through "The Gift"—a song in which Buffy says goodbye to her sister before making the ultimate sacrifice—without crying.

The last song of our encore that night was our old standby "Teacher's Pet," a tune for which, you may recall, Kristin traditionally dons a praying mantis mask and dances about in a mantisesque manner. We wanted to kick things up a notch for this last hurrah, so we'd sent up a flare in the Scoobyverse to enlist a mantis army of sorts, with the intention of buying rubber masks for anyone who volunteered as tribute. But we were shocked to discover that, perhaps due to the various supply chain challenges that had cropped up in recent years, the masks had become prohibitively expensive.

However, just as we knew each other's love languages, we also knew the love language of our listeners: making magical things happen for fun, because fun rules! We knew exactly whom to contact about assembling a covert mantis mask-crafting army: LaRena, a Brooklyn-based crafter who'd come to many *Buffering* shows with gifts she'd handmade for us over the years. "LaRena, we need a mantis army big enough to make an impact but small enough to remain a surprise for most of the audience." Within a week, LaRena had contacted twenty *Buffering* Scoobies and they gathered both virtually and in person at her apartment to snip, trim, and glue bits of green felt and giant bobble eyes together to create mantis masks a hundred times more incredible than any we could have purchased. As Jenny sang about the mandibles and serrated hands of Ms. French, Kristin performed her now-signature move of opening and closing her claws (hands), and this served as the signal for our crew to don their creations and swarm the stage for our big finish.

It ruled.

The next night, the atmosphere was positively electric at The Bell House. The house lights came down and our traditional intro video—*Buffy*'s opening credits edited to include both of us and our special guests in the cast lineup—played on the massive projector screen overhead. As the theme song blasted through speakers, we both stood together just offstage, peering out at the audience as they began their second evening of whooping, screaming, and chanting, and were overwhelmed by the whole big wild vampire-themed family we'd made together.

We burst onto the stage, dancing and running loops around the table before finally sitting down. Jenny choked on her customary opening phrase, "Hello and welcome to *Buffering the Vampire Slayer*," as we both blinked back tears.

As you might imagine, a lot happens in the last episode of *Buffy the Vampire Slayer*. A great battle is nigh! The residents of Sunnydale—who have weathered demons and apocalypses aplenty—are finally fleeing from what seems to be the capital-A *Apocalypse*. The town, soon to be swallowed by the Hellmouth, is empty apart from our Slayers, our Watcher, our Scoobies, our Potentials, and the First Evil.

Buffy brings a new, mystical weapon back to Slayer headquarters. Mostly referred to in-series as the Scythe, the weapon is actually a three-way hybrid between an axe, a scythe, and a stake, and it contains an immense power previously hidden away from the Slayer line. Buffy calls a meeting with Willow, Faith, Xander, Dawn, and Giles and explains a new plan to this core group of Scoobies, a plan that makes Xander ask if she is, in any way, kidding, and one that Giles calls "bloody brilliant."

Inside The Bell House, we talked through the speech that

Buffy had given to a room full of potential Slayers. We were reciting it to a room full of hundreds of *Buffy* fans, while hundreds more watched from home. Once more we found ourselves in a familiar place: that spot in the Venn diagram where *Buffy* and *Buffering* so beautifully overlapped.

Kristin spoke the first lines Buffy delivers to the Potentials: "Here's the part where you make a choice."

The crowd cried out, and Jenny reassured everyone in the room that they would be okay—we would make it through this! We all took a deep, steadying breath together, and Kristin continued:

"In every generation, one Slayer is born, because a bunch of men who died thousands of years ago made up that rule."

On cue, the crowd booed and hissed, then scream-sang along as we (also on cue) played the Patriarchy jingle.[4]

Back at the Summers home, Buffy continues explaining her plan. "They were powerful men," she says, and then, gesturing to Willow, "This woman is more powerful than all of them combined."

At this point in Brooklyn, Kristin was pausing after each sentence as the crowd grew louder, some stomping their feet, others whooping. Many held each other tightly.

"So I say we change the rule. I say that my power should be our power. To change our destiny. From now on, every girl in the world who might be a Slayer—"

---

4 In addition to our episodic songs, we created a collection of jingles—shorter pieces of music deployed in-episode to shout out characters we love (Cordelia!), tropes we hate (the patriarchy!), or recurring themes in our own conversations (yes, we have a Hellmath jingle).

Without prompting, every person inside The Bell House shouted in unison, "*will* be a Slayer!"

All four hundred of us spoke the rest of Buffy's words in unison:

Who *could* have the power, *will* have the power.
Who *can* stand up, *will* stand up.
Slayers, every one of us.
Make your choice.
Are you ready to be strong?

+⁺⋅⋆⁚

At the new Sunnydale High School, the principal's office sits directly above the Hellmouth. This is where Willow and a Potential named Kennedy (who, incidentally, is also Willow's new girlfriend) sit down together; Willow, holding the Scythe, begins working the immense magic needed to accomplish Buffy's plan as the Potentials descend onto the battleground below with Buffy and Faith.

As Willow completes her spell, it is clear from the faces of the Potentials inside the Hellmouth that the gambit is a success. Somewhere else in the world, a young girl steps up to home plate, baseball bat in hand, a shadow of uncertainty falling across her face. Then a series of other young women around the world flash across the screen, each experiencing the sudden, overwhelming influx of Slayer power. We end once again on the batter, who is now staring down the camera with a look of certainty. She is going to demolish that baseball.

Ultimately, Buffy is able to overcome the greatest obstacle she has ever faced by doing what no Slayer before her has done:

sharing her power. By transforming the Potentials into Slayers, she transcends her status of Chosen One and becomes instead a Chosen One of Many. This is the lesson we learn again and again in *Buffy*, but never so clearly or on so grand a scale as at the end of the series: We are stronger together. We are *better* together.

At the end of "Chosen," Buffy and those who remain standing look out over the gaping canyon that was once Sunnydale. They have discovered the power found in a chosen family over the past seven seasons, and they have held each other up amidst some of life's most brutal blows. Together, they saved the world a lot. But we aren't still talking about this story decades later because they saved the *world*. The Slayer and her friends stay in our hearts and our brains and our blood because, over and over and over again, they saved each other.

We were married to each other when we began *Buffering the Vampire Slayer*, which some might consider the ultimate measure of togetherness. Along the way, we changed, as people tend to do, and so did the nature of our relationship. When it became clear in the wake of our separation that we planned to keep working together, a lot of our closest friends urged us to reconsider. This couldn't be healthy, right? We also wrestled with this question ourselves. But we chose to do the unthinkable for two reasons: because we wanted to remain in community with our incredible Scoobies and because even though we knew we hadn't been in the right *kind* of relationship, we still missed each other when we were in no relationship at all. And so we continued copiloting our funny little ship through innumerable storms both public and private, holding it (and ourselves) together with hope, laughter, and sheer will.

At The Bell House, many of the faces we could see beaming

up at us were faces we'd seen in every season that had come before; over the years, they'd shown us reflections of ourselves that allowed us to see who we could be to each other.

We ended the episode by singing a very appropriately named song from *Once More with Once More, with Feeling*: "The End of the Episode," followed by a version of our signature sign-off. In the 143 episodes that had preceded this one, Jenny would signal the end of the episode by saying, "And 'til next time . . . ," and then we'd both say, "Awoooooooo."

That night Jenny said, "And for the *last* time . . . ," and we all howled out together.

CHOSEN

Seems like only yesterday and a hundred years ago
That I first put my foot down
   on this ground I've come to know

Came to this town and I looked all around
Thought that I was alone but I never was

Cause you've been here as long as I can say
Shining so bright, you carry the light
And you'll hold fast forever and a day
Deep in my heart, chasing the dark away

They told me that this fight I found
   was mine and mine alone
That the haunted path before me
   I'd have to walk all on my own

Came to this town and I got kicked around
Thought that I was alone but I never was

Cause you've been here as long as I can say
Shining so bright, you carry the light
And you'll hold fast forever and a day
Deep in my heart, chasing the dark away

Seems like only yesterday and a hundred years ago
That my entire life got changed when we first said hello

epilogue

NO PLACE LIKE HOME

At the end of the seventh season, Sunnydale has been swallowed up by the Hellmouth, but Buffy and many of her closest remain standing; we don't know where they're headed (apart from Dawn, who will be searching for the nearest mall), but we do know that they will continue doing what they do, beyond Sunnydale. There will be more battles to fight, more lessons to learn, more loves, and undoubtedly more losses. The same was true for us. If *Buffering* was our Sunnydale, we were now watching the battered "Welcome to . . ." sign shrink slowly in our rearview mirror as we too headed somewhere *beyond*.

If it was hard for you to believe that we'd wrap up our seven-season run through *Buffy* on the very same stage where we'd married back in 2013, then you'll surely think we're lying when we tell you that on the very same weekend of our finale, in that very same venue, Kristin met someone to whom she would be married in one year's time. Avanthi was a friend of Jenny and Jess, a tour manager by trade who agreed to come to Brooklyn for a few days to ensure that our finale ship would sail smoothly into the sunset. No one—Kristin perhaps least of all—expected that she would ask Avanthi to go on a date with her later that same month . . . in *Nashville*, where Avanthi lived. The fact that Avanthi was not scared off by Kristin's willingness to fly from New York to Tennessee for a first date should have been a sign to all that they were a good match. They were such a good match, in fact, that Kristin would then quadruple her first-date flying time to surprise Avanthi in Tokyo six months after their first date with a marriage proposal.

Meanwhile, just three months after we howled our final wolf howl together, Jenny and Jess welcomed a tiny son named Alderic into their home and hearts. What he lacked in street smarts and cash flow he more than made up for in coos, blinks, and general adorableness, from the top of his fuzzy coconut head to the tips of his teeny tiny toes. Caring for a baby has little in common with making a podcast but rather a great deal in common with vampire slaying: there's never a dull moment, you must complete delicate tasks whilst shrouded in total darkness, and you are constantly at the mercy of a being whose number one priority is their unquenchable thirst for life-giving liquids. Some might say Jenny had been preparing for this adventure for years.

Clearly, with a fresh baby in the mix and an imminent wedding looming on the horizon, it was time for us to take a niiiiiice long break from work. *cue audience laugh track*

Only a month after Kristin's Tokyo proposal and just shy of Alderic's three-month birthday, Kristin arrived on Jess and Jenny's doorstep in Maine to begin not one but *two* new projects.

The first was this book. Kristin spent a week in an Airbnb two blocks from Jenny's house as we began the process of writing together. While we had previous experience podcasting together, making music together, and solving crossword puzzles together, the prospect of writing a whole *book* felt considerably more daunting. Once again, we had to learn something new.

Jenny took it upon herself to bring a copy of Anne Lamott's *Bird by Bird* over to Kristin's rental each morning. The apartment had a gas fireplace, so Jenny would enter the living room with a degree of dramatic flourish usually reserved for folks in smoking jackets, click the fireplace remote (grinning wildly to herself as the flames ignited), clear her throat meaningfully, and read aloud the next chapter of the book. Kristin would dutifully listen, staring into the fire as well, or out across the backyard where horses (wearing little jackets!!) frolicked on a hillside. We both benefited deeply from Anne's reminders about shitty first drafts, as even in the earliest days we would find ourselves spending hours on the crafting of a single paragraph.

Outside of the writing, the other new project we set to work on was *The eX-Files*. Our next rewatch podcast adventure would give Jenny the opportunity to show Kristin another one of her favorite nineties shows for the first time (*The X-Files*, of course!) and also allow us the deep satisfaction of playing on our status as mutual ex-wives in the title.

Our recordings look a little different now. We take breaks when Alderic wakes up from his naps, and Kristin often yells to Avanthi to come join her on the Zoom call when Jenny takes the phone into his bedroom to join Jess, Frank, and a tiny toddling (as of this writing) baby. Alderic delights us all with new tricks such as saying "hi!" and squishing his little hands together; Frank rolls around in the background, occasionally coming up to boop the camera with his nose; and we catch up on small life things. We periodically indulge in remote group watches of movies from the *Twilight* franchise together (the slope between "it's a joke" and "seriously, when are we watching *New Moon*" is a slippery one indeed). Jess is the group's lone member of Team Edward, Avanthi loves Bella's dad, Jenny loves Bella's dad's flannels, and Kristin can never get over how *anyone* could be Team Edward.

The green chair that Kristin sat in the day we recorded our pilot episode in the Altadena home now sits in Jess and Jenny's living room in Maine. On a recent Christmas, Jenny's mom told her that she'd purchased the chair in 1977. The wooden desk that held the computer in that original recording studio setup, also purchased in the late seventies by Kristin's parents, now sits in Avanthi's office in upstate New York.

Time is weird. Life is weird. But due in no small part to a certain Slayer, and due in no small part to an amazing community of Scoobies who loved her, and then us . . . against incredible odds, we still get to be weird together.

appendix a

HELLMATH, CONTINUED

B *uffering*'s Scoobies were a roving force of nature when it came to picking up the baton of Hellmath and running with it. Below is a sampling of some of our very favorite listener-submitted Hellmathian applications.

Flammable Vampires and Other Delights

According to lore, the greatest threats to a vampire's health and safety are sunlight, a stake through the heart, decapitation, and fire. Yet despite the inherent danger, Angel seems to spend nearly all of his free time either (1) lounging near a roaring fireplace, (2) reading a leather-bound copy of Sartre's *Nausea* in the original French by candelabra light, or (3) both at once. His seeming indifference to the perils of hanging around near open flame gave us reason to track this behavior; we dubbed our ongoing study "Immolation Watch."

However, a listener named Michelle wrote in to offer a compelling argument as to why Angel might be much more comfortable around fire than vampires sired in more recent years:

> For the past couple of episodes you've gotten very heated about Angel's love of fire, despite it being one of his weaknesses, and I'm here to fight for him using HELLMATH.
>
> Angel was sired in 1753 and electric lights weren't invented until the 1880s, however it wasn't until 1925 when electric power was commonly used in most homes. 1753–1925 = 172 years between his siring and electric light. Season 3 is set in 1998, which means that Angel has only been using electricity for 73 years. Before then, Angel was using fireplaces, candles, gas lamps, etc. to light his homes.
>
> In addition, he probably built plenty of fires when he was mortal, let's say 16 years experience (26 years old when sired, probably started building fires on his own around 10 years old = 16 years) and he was in Acathla's Hell Hole for about a century, which I imagine to be pretty fiery. Therefore, our brooding, eyeliner wearing, dreamboat has been working those flames for a long ass time and can handle himself just fine, thank you.

If You Can't Be with the One You Glove, Glove the One You're With

In Season 3, Episode 7, "Revelations," a woman by the name of Gwendolyn Post arrives in Sunnydale claiming to be Faith's Watcher. We learn as the episode progresses that Gwendolyn Post is *actually* a big evil liar who has *actually* infiltrated Buffy's

Scooby gang to get her hands on (or perhaps we should say, to get her hand *in*) the
Glove of Myhnegon, a powerful and dan-
gerous weapon.

As the episode-ending battle for the
Glove intensifies (with Gwendolyn actually
getting it onto her grimy little hand!), Buffy
picks up a shard of broken glass from the floor and
hurls it across the room, separating Gwendolyn from
her newfound power (and also her entire arm).

We asked our listeners, "Can you *do* that? Can you
throw a piece of glass so hard that it cuts through muscle, bone,
and whatever else you have inside your arm?"

Two days later, we received an email from a listener named
Grace, a graduate student in the Walker Group at Montana
State University.

Hi Kristin and Jenny,

I'm listening to the podcast episode where you discuss if it's
feasible for Buffy to have sliced off Gwendolyn Post's arm
with the bit of glass from the ceiling. I decided to do the
math to see how that works out.

Short answer is—probably not possible, even at the far
limits of reasonable values for the mass of a glass piece and
how fast Buffy could throw it.

The equation of concern here is Newton's second law
of motion: $F = ma$. We need to see if the force (F) required
to break a bone, which I'm assuming is the greatest barrier to
slicing an arm clean off, is a force that can be exerted by
a piece of glass thrown across a room. According to Michi-
gan State University, the minimum force required to break
a bone is about 3200 Newtons (N).

Looking at the glass piece that Buffy threw, I'm estimating that it is about 7 inches (17.76 cm) in diameter and is roughly circular. To find the mass of the glass, we need to know the volume of the glass piece and its density. Volume is easy—for a cylinder V = pi*r^2*h. If I assume a diameter of 17.76 cm, the radius (r) is 8.89 cm. According to the internet, the width (h) of a standard pane of glass can vary anywhere from 3–6 mm. Using the higher end of that estimate (h = 6 mm), we find that the volume of the piece of glass Buffy threw is roughly 150 cm^3 (maximum). To find the mass of this volume of glass, we need to know the density of the glass. That varies, but the maximum value, even for the heaviest leaded glass, is about 8 g/cm^3. Using that value, that would give the glass a mass of 1200 g or 1.2 kg.

Now that we have the mass, we need to know how fast Buffy threw it. If you guess from the floor plan of the episode, that piece of glass crossed about 50 ft of space in about 2 seconds, which puts the velocity when it hit Gwendolyn Post at 25 ft/s or 7.62 m/s. On the other hand, if you assume that as the Slayer, Buffy can throw that piece of glass as fast as the fastest pitcher on Earth, we can take its velocity when it hits to be ~100 mph or 44.7 m/s. Using the higher value and a 2 second crossing from Buffy to Gwendolyn, the acceleration when it hits would be 22.35 m/s^2.

Given both a mass and an acceleration, we find that the force with which the piece of glass hits Gwendolyn is 26.8 N, or roughly 100x too small a force to effectively sever a limb.

You've Heard of Hell*math*, but Have You Considered Hellproperty Law?

In Season 6, Buffy—newly risen from the grave—has inherited her family home. We wondered aloud on the podcast: If a vampire has been invited into a home, but then the house is sold, at what point does the existing invitation become invalid, effectively resetting the threshold for undead visitors? We each happened to be in the process of buying a home at the time, so our brains provided fertile ground for the minutiae of property law and vampire rules to commingle. Lucky for us, listener Stacy was ready at the keyboard:

> Hi Kristin and Jenny, I'm a first year law student currently studying for my property final, and a question you mused on in the "Flooded" episode has stuck in my mind—At what point in the sale of a house can a previously invited-in vampire no longer enter? When does it reset? I decided to think about this as a fun hypothetical practice question in the process of my studying. I think an argument could be made that a vampire can no longer come inside in the gap period (or executory period) between the signing of the sales contract and the closing.
>
> The doctrine of equitable conversion says that at the moment the sales contract is signed, the purchaser attains a real property interest in the property in the form of equitable title, and the seller now has only a personal property interest (although they do still have legal title to the property). This has many possible consequences, such as requiring that the purchaser (rather than the seller) bear the risk of loss for damages to the property. Another consequence is that when a party in a joint tenancy with right of survivorship signs a sale contract

to sell their interest, the joint tenancy is severed. The doc-
trine of equitable conversion is only a default rule and many
jurisdictions have imposed stricter or looser requirements on
it, but I think that it makes enough of a difference to result
in a decent argument that the vampire invitation could reset
itself at the gap/executory period, not
just closing.

We also kept a regular stream
of our own Hellmathian theorems flowing throughout the
podcast, including such equa-
tions as:

If a gathering leaves the sta-
tion traveling northeast at sixty-five miles an hour and a shin-
dig leaves the opposite station heading southwest at fifty-five
miles an hour, when do they crash and create a hootenanny?
    —Season 3, Episode 2, "Dead Man's Party"

If a coffin is approximately two feet in height, then Buffy
and Dawn would need seven coffins stacked on top of each
other to create the height needed to escape the graveyard

sinkhole—approximated at fifteen feet in total depth—where they are trapped.

—Season 6, Episode 22, "Grave"

Villains are bad. Villains love milk. Therefore, milk is bad.

—Season 7, Episode 18, "Dirty Girls"

But to share every last precious equation, discovery, and hypothesis with you, dear reader, would require a whole separate book.

appendix b

BEHIND THE SCENES WITH THE CAST OF BUFFY

At the start of the podcast, we couldn't have imagined speaking to anyone from the cast. We were just two girls! Who would want to talk to us?! Jenny had a friend named Steven Smith, though, who had appeared in the first season of *Buffy*. He'd played a high school student in two episodes, most notably delivering a few speaking lines in the Sunnydale High computer lab in "The Harvest," when Willow tricks Cordelia into deleting her entire term paper.[1] Steven had a podcast of his own, *Going Off Track*, that Jenny had been a guest on the year prior, so we felt comfortable enough to ask him to come on *Buffering*. He was our very first interview, and, in addition to telling us the tales of his experience on set, he also imparted a very crucial piece of podcasting wisdom: "When it comes to interviewing the cast and creators of the show," he said, "ask *everyone*."

---

1 Hilariously, the decision was made during the editing stage that Steven's voice should sound more "surfery," and his lines were overdubbed by another actor; evidence that in 1997, we were all living in a post–Breckin Meyer world.

Not everyone said yes; heck, not everyone even responded. But a surprising number did. We talked to a *literal* murderer's row of gods and vampires: Clare Kramer (Glory) told us about her habit of collecting chairs—so many that she had to use her garage for overflow; Mercedes McNab (Harmony) graciously agreed to say "Blondie Bear," one of her most beloved pet names for Spike, on mic at a studio in San Francisco; Juliet Landau (Drusilla) hypnotized us with the story of her chemistry read with James Marsters; James (Spike) in turn spent an afternoon with us telling us about his roots in theater and how Anthony Head (Giles) had worked with him on Spike's British accent.

We spoke with Sharon Ferguson (Sineya, the first Slayer) and learned that she had a long career working with the Artist Formerly Known as Prince. As if that weren't enough, she also showed us her *six-foot bullwhip*—a gift from the stunt coordinator on *Catwoman,* who'd then taught Sharon how to use it! Kristin flew all the way down to Atlanta to chat with stunt coordinator Jeff Pruitt and stunt performer Sophia Crawford, who worked together to create all of Buffy's risky moves in the first several seasons of the show; she interviewed them in the coffeeshop they'd opened together, setting up a mobile recording rig on one of the café tables after the shop had closed for the day. We were gifted the *actual* first-season script from *Buffy*'s music supervisor, marked up in the margins with all manner of delightful on-set commentary. Both Jeff Kober (Kralik, Rack) and Harry Groener (the Mayor) came over to our home to record their interviews in our basement studio; Jeff surprised us with a moving conversation about his spirituality and meditation practice, and Harry delighted us when he autographed our replica of Faith's knife.[2] We crammed our

---

2 A thing of beauty, boss!

bodies into a postinterview photo booth with frickin' Seth Green!

What follows are some of our favorite moments with the wonderful folks who worked to bring us *Buffy*.

The One Where the Cheese Man Cometh

There's a character in the Season 4 finale of *Buffy* who appears in the dreams of Giles, Buffy, Willow, and Xander. He walks slowly into frame in each of their wildly chaotic dreamscapes— *Buffy* is truly one of the best shows at capturing just how strange and emotional and topsy-turvy a dreamscape can be— and offers them slices of glistening, golden American cheese. In Willow's dream he says only, "I've made a little space for the cheese slices," and he tells Giles, "I wear the cheese. It does not wear me." He explains to Xander that the cheese will not protect him, and in Buffy's dream, he simply waggles the cheese meaningfully in the air before retreating.

In April 2019, with a number of cast interviews under our belt but many more still to come, we met with David Wells, the actor who portrayed the enigmatic Cheese Man. We had a blast chatting, and he was clearly tickled by the fact that for the last twenty years he's been approached on the street, and in restaurants, and at the grocery store, by scores of people who recognized him from (we assume) the oddest role he ever played. Our custom at the end of an interview was to take a group selfie (provided the interviewee was game). The photos from this day—all three of us grinning while holding up individually wrapped Kraft singles to the camera—really capture the wild essence of what it often felt like when we found ourselves in the company of the folks who helped make *Buffy* so singular and so special.

The One Where We Explain *Buffy* to the Cast of *Buffy*

When we went to the Vampire Ball in London, one of the highlights was the costume contest. The competition was open to all convention attendees, and a bevy of *Buffy* cast members sat on the panel of judges. Somehow, amidst this *Buffy* royalty, we too were invited to judge. While there were scores of amazing entries, one individual in particular blew our minds, wearing a homemade "Buffy Will Patrol Tonight" outfit. The costume was a faithful re-creation of a doodle made by Giles in Season 4's "Hush" (the very same doodle, you may recall, that Isabella Rotman replicated for our finale gifts!) in which the Slayer is depicted (poorly) with a bow in one hand and an arrow in the other, and the titular directive re: patrolling scrawled above her unintentionally asymmetrical hairstyle. There is something hilarious about seeing a depiction of the Chosen One, who regularly deals with matters of life, death, and apocalypse, rendered at a skill level approximately one notch above "stick figure." Though instantly recognizable as a re-creation of Giles's drawing to most in the fandom, this masterpiece was totally baffling to the cast members onstage with us. Of those present, only James Marsters was in the episode, and he did not appear in the iconic overhead projector scene that inspired the costume. As we hooted, guffawed, and clapped in delight, James and Juliet Landau leaned over to whisper-ask what they were missing. We rushed to explain as the competitors finished their walks down the aisle. "So, in this episode everyone in Sunnydale loses their *voice* because these extremely creepy fairytale monsters called *the Gentlemen* are collecting *hearts* in *jars* and so everyone in the Scooby gang assembles in an empty college lecture hall, and Giles has to *draw out* the plan using *transparencies* and it is epically funny, and this is what Buffy looks like on one of the slides!!!" At first, just James and Juliet leaned in to listen as we breathlessly recounted the events of the episode. But by the time we reached the end of our synopsis, the whole judges' table—including Tom Lenk (Andrew), Brian Thompson (Luke, the Judge), Andrew J. Ferchland (the Anointed One), and Mark Metcalf (the Master)—had tuned in to hear us explain the plotline. We genuinely could not have imagined the bizarre set of circumstances that had led us to contextualizing an iconic image from *Buffy* to the actors who *literally made the show.*

The One Where Nerf Herder Gives Us Our Very Own Piece of the Hellmouth

You know that feeling when you are covering a television series set in the fictional town of Sunnydale, California, that is allegedly meant to be Santa Barbara, California, and then you receive an email *from the actual mayor* of Santa Barbara, who invites you to her city to prove to you once and for all that Sunnydale is *actually* Santa Barbara? We know this feeling, friends, because this is what happened to us.

The note, sent from Mayor Helene Schneider and three of her close friends (self-described as "a group of kick-ass, progressive, politically active women of varied sexual orientations who fight the patriarchy and have bonded over our mutual love of *Buffy the Vampire Slayer*"), urged us to drive north, where they would take us on a tour of their city, showing us the many places that overlapped precisely with scenes in the television show. All of this happened right as we were set to begin our third season, in which the Big Bad is none other than *the mayor of Sunnydale*. How could we say no?

As planning commenced, Mayor Helene wrote to tell us of more good news: in addition to the guided tour that was being curated for our arrival, she'd also asked Nerf Herder—the band, also based in Santa Barbara, who wrote and performed the theme song that was used for all seven seasons of *Buffy*—if they'd sit down and chat with us, and they'd said yes!

When we arrived, we met up at the home of one of our hosts. As we pulled into the driveway, we saw a large banner hanging above the garage—an exact replica of the WELCOME TO SUNNYDALE sign! After initial hellos, our hosts gave us a handmade book that listed, scene by scene, the irrefutable proof that Sunnydale was indeed meant to be Santa Barbara. Following the book's itinerary, they drove us to a lookout point and held up a photo of Angel in "Amends," drawing our attention to where the terrain line in the photo matched up with the still. Next, they brought us to a rooftop downtown, then produced a printout of a familiar B-roll shot of "Sunnydale," which now came to life before our very eyes. They took us to a number of places that seemed to be real-life analogues to consequential locations in *Buffy*: the docks, the zoo, a rose garden where, they suggested, Angelus may have obtained the roses he used to traumatize Giles in the Season 2 episode "Passion." In addition to the Sunnydale tour stops, Mayor Helene also let us go into the mayor's office (no lukewarm milk or sanitizing hand wipes were found) and permitted us to bang the gavel in the room where government officials gathered.

The final stop on our tour: a sit-down with two of the members of Nerf Herder, Parry Gripp and Steve Sherlock. You won't be surprised to learn that our incredible quartet of Santa

Barbara enthusiasts had created yet another custom banner for the second half of the day: the sign that hangs outside the Bronze—Sunnydale's favorite (only?) teen dance club. Parry and Steve sat down to tell us a bunch of incredibly fun stories, including when they first learned their song was being used as the *Buffy* theme, which was, if you can believe it, *the day the pilot aired on TV,* and the time they ran into Julie Benz (Darla) on set . . . in full vamp face. Toward the end of the interview, we asked them about being the last band to ever play the Bronze.[3] Steve explained that after shooting that performance, they'd simply wandered around the set of the show. "We had free rein of the entire set. Nobody cared! We did whatever we wanted. We were playing with the props, going from room to room, we even sat on the couch where Joyce died." (At this point in the telling we cried out in agony, "TOO SOON!") They spent time literally raiding the dumpsters, as the massive set of the Hellmouth was being torn up. Steve reached under the table and, to punctuate his story, revealed a massive, speckled piece of Styrofoam. We gasped. He'd brought with him a piece of the *actual Hellmouth.* We wowed. We actually clapped. Steve and Parry were so moved by our response that, after we finished recording, they ceremoniously broke off one small corner of their Hellmouth and gifted it to us.[4]

---

3 In addition to being Sunnydale's most popular (and only) dance club, the Bronze hosted live performances by many musical acts—including Michelle Branch, Aimee Mann, and the Breeders. *Beverly Hills, 90210* had the Peach Pit, and Sunnydale had the Bronze!

4 Later, when we got divorced, we followed California state law and split our allotment of the Hellmouth into equal halves, allowing us each to maintain custody.

The One with Principal Snyder and the Presidential Election

Armin Shimerman was the first major cast member we invited onto the podcast, and when he agreed, we squealed in our Altadena home together at our good fortune. Armin portrayed Principal Snyder, the strict head of Sunnydale High School from the middle of Season 1 (following the untimely demise of Snyder's predecessor) until the end of Season 3 (upon the occasion of Snyder's own untimely demise). We had the interview scheduled for November 7, 2016. That this was the day after the presidential election did not really occur to us until the evening of November 6, which Jenny spent numbly staring at her computer screen in the studio and Kristin spent chain-smoking in the backyard. So when we woke up the next day puffy-eyed and bleary, we guessed that—given our newfound national circumstances—Armin would cancel.

He did not.

After we said our introductory hellos, the three of us immediately began talking about the election. As we'd come to find out, nearly every conversation we'd have in the immediate future with anyone in our lives (including many of the cast members of *Buffy*) would mirror this format; we couldn't have a "regular" conversation without first engaging in a new protocol of sociopolitical processing that was equal parts rage purge and wellness check. Armin happened to be deep into political organizing already, rallying the *Star Trek* community to vote (he played the beloved Ferengi barkeep Quark on *Deep Space Nine* from 1993 to 1999).

Once we'd purged and checked with Armin, we talked about behind-the-scenes tidbits from the set of *Buffy*. He told us how he'd originally auditioned for the role of Principal Flutie, didn't get the part, but was then cast as Snyder after Flutie was devoured by a group of students possessed by the spirits of hyenas. Early on, he was told that his character's arc would be brief, given the short life expectancy of school administrators on the Hellmouth, but he ended up remaining on the show for the next two seasons. He told us about the skepticism he felt upon learning he'd be sharing scenes with a then-nineteen Sarah Michelle Gellar, whose most notable previous work had been on the daytime soap opera *All My Children*. That skepticism was killed off faster than Principal Flutie, thanks to Gellar's immense talent and infamous work ethic, but he channeled that initial skepticism into Snyder's treatment of Buffy and the other students at Sunnydale High.

The One Where We Come Out in Italian to Kristine Sutherland

During our third season, we had the absolute privilege and honor of talking with Kristine Sutherland, who plays Buffy's mom, Joyce Summers. We had situated the interview to pair with one of the most iconic Joyce episodes in the series, "Band Candy," in which Joyce and Giles (along with, to everyone's chagrin, Principal Snyder) revert to their teenage selves. We chatted about her experience in that episode—the cop car! the bubblegum! the *handcuffs*!—and of course also spent time talking about Season 5's "The Body."

But our favorite moment from the conversation came during our discussion of Season 2's final episode, "Becoming."

For the entire show, up to this point, Buffy has led a double life, keeping her Slayer identity a secret, most notably from her mom. When events suddenly require this wall to come down and Joyce to learn the truth, we (along with many in the fandom) couldn't help but feel a sense of déjà vu. Joyce asks Buffy if she's *sure*, if she's tried *not* being the Slayer, and if perhaps her lack of a strong father figure may have played a part in all this. We'd heard some of these exact same phrases from our own mothers in the 1990s—though of course we'd come out as something a bit different from a vampire Slayer (less garlic, more flannel).

As we talked together about this scene and its resonance for so many, Kristine wanted to learn more about *our* coming-out experiences and about Kristin's work in LGBTQ advocacy. Not for the last time, the interviewers became the interviewees. *Buffy* alums seem especially skilled at this pivot. Kristin told Kristine about the book she'd published just a handful of years earlier called *This Is a Book for Parents of Gay Kids*, and Kristine in turn shared an experience she was having with a family in Italy (where she resides for half the year). A young girl who lived a few doors down had recently come out to her parents, and they were having a difficult time. She said she thought they'd love to have a resource like this book, if only it were available in Italian. Incredibly, the book had only been translated into two languages outside of English: Japanese, and . . . *friggin' Italian.*

Before we ended our conversation we exchanged information, and that week Kristin sent two of the Italian-language copies over to Kristine, who flew them back to Italy. In lieu of having a *This Is a Book for Parents of Slayers* guidebook for Joyce back in 1998, we figured this was the least we could do.

The One Where Charisma Carpenter Sleuths

The character of Cordelia is one of the most beloved in our *Buffering* universe. She inspired the very first of our jingles, ethereal harp pluckings that surround the lyrical refrain "Cordelia, you're perfect. Cordelia, I love you." She was the high school mean girl who started as a privileged bully and slowly peeled back her outer layers to reveal a complex, fierce, generous badass of a woman.

So even though it was only a month before Kristin would fly from New York to Los Angeles to sign divorce paperwork, run into James Van Der Beek, and smoosh into a photo booth with Seth Green, she crossed the country without hesitation when Charisma Carpenter agreed to an in-person interview.

Charisma met up with us at Headgum's warehouse-esque studio space in downtown Los Angeles. She was an instantly disarming presence. Moments after settling into a corner of the studio couch, she told us how excited she was to finally meet us ("to meet *us*?!" our brains screeched) and explained that at many of the cons she'd attended over the past few years, fans had played her our Cordelia jingle (thanks, guys). She then told us, as though it was the most normal thing in the universe, that she had liked the jingle so much that she had made it a ringtone and assigned it to the contacts in her phone whom she'd worked with on *Buffy* and *Angel*. "So if Greenie calls"—that's David Greenwalt to you, bub!—"your jingle plays!!"

We were astounded, and years later, we remain astounded.

Somehow, though, this was not the moment in our conversation that awed us the most! Charisma was incredibly generous with her time and sat with us for nearly two hours. She told us how she'd had to leave the set of *Malibu Shores* to go to her *Buffy* audition, which meant a drive from Long Beach to Burbank (giving us a classic Californian rundown of taking the 405 to the 710 to the 101, of course). She convinced the costume department to let her stay in her costume so she could make the call time, but then of course was stuck in traffic in her Nissan Sentra. This was before most of us had cell phones, and Charisma was included: she only had her beeper, and as the time went by her agent paged her several times until she finally pulled off to call her back on a payphone.

She explained, "I dial my agent and I'm like, 'What's up?' She's like, 'Where are you? They want to leave. They're starving.' I go, 'You tell them to order a large pizza because I've been in traffic for an hour and they are going to see me.' Like who says that?"

In unison we both replied, "CORDELIA!"

Needless to say, the folks at the Warner Bros. Ranch did wait, and before Charisma had even made it back to her apartment, she had secured the role.

Toward the end of the conversation, we were talking about making the podcast from our remote locations in New York and Los Angeles. Charisma looked at us, her expression a mix of confusion and interest. With the directness that Cordelia herself is most known for, she asked, "Wait, what is going on here—were you two together?"

We exploded into laughter and explained to her that we had started the podcast when we were married to each other, and that after nearly ten years together we had decided to separate. Charisma, just like everyone else, could not believe that we were still able to make the podcast. She thought for a moment and then said, "It's like my ex-husband and I are raising our child together, coparenting separately. You're kind of doing that. This is your baby and you guys are coparenting and doing this together. That's amazing."

Nothing like starting a podcast with your wife about *Buffy* and then, a few years later, explaining your divorce to one of the biggest stars of the show. That's . . . show business, baby?

appendix c

CHORD SHEETS

From the Desk of Jenny Owen Youngs:
Liner Notes

HELLO! Jenny here!

When I came up with the idea to make original music part of *Buffering the Vampire Slayer*, it never occurred to me that people listening to the show might one day be interested in learning how to *play* those songs. It was a lovely surprise when folks started emailing and leaving comments, asking about the chords for this song or that song. I started making chord sheets that included the lyrics, the chords I was using, and a doodle here and there for good measure. For your strumming and plucking enjoyment, we've decided to include a handful of our favorites here. Good journey!

Angel

"Angel" was the first song in our catalog to delve deep into feelings territory, rather than monster-of-the-week fare. It was a turning point in the music of *Buffering,* and I approached the lyrics the same way I would have if I'd been writing the song for myself, following the thread of Buffy's emotions.

Even after she discovers the truth about Angel's murderous past, Buffy cannot suppress her growing feelings for this man who should, according to her sacred calling, be at the top of her kill list. She sees the man he is trying to be rather than the monster he has been.

Buffy composer Christophe Beck created a heart-wrenching love theme for Buffy and Angel called "Close Your Eyes." Knowing the rocky road that still lay ahead for these star-crossed lovers, it seemed fitting that we should create a love theme of our own. And so a small melodic figure was born, which I tried to infuse with wistfulness and yearning; it first appeared in "Angel," and went on to be reprised in subsequent songs dealing with the emotionally heavy Bangel relationship episodes: "Surprise," "Innocence," "Becoming," and both iterations of "I Will Remember You."

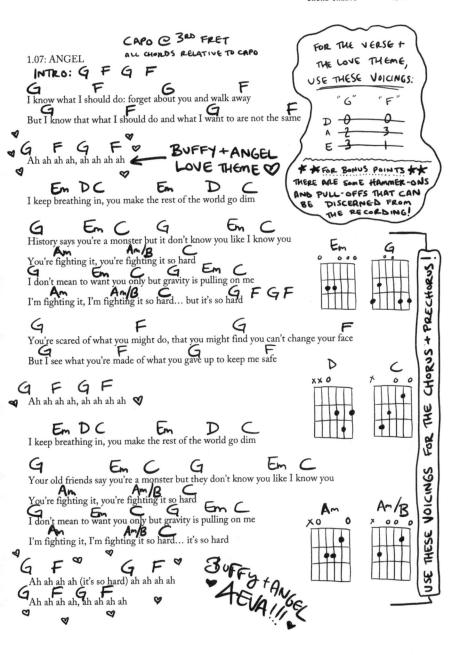

1.07: ANGEL

CAPO @ 3RD FRET
ALL CHORDS RELATIVE TO CAPO

INTRO: G F G F

G   F   G   F
I know what I should do: forget about you and walk away

G   F   G   F
But I know that what I should do and what I want to are not the same

G   F   G   F
Ah ah ah ah, ah ah ah ah   BUFFY + ANGEL
                                  LOVE THEME ♥

    Em D C   Em   D   C
I keep breathing in, you make the rest of the world go dim

G   Em   C   G   Em   C
History says you're a monster but it don't know you like I know you

    Am   Am/B   C
You're fighting it, you're fighting it so hard

G   Em   C   G   Em   C
I don't mean to want you only but gravity is pulling on me

    Am   Am/B   C   G F G F
I'm fighting it, I'm fighting it so hard... but it's so hard

G   F   G   F
You're scared of what you might do, that you might find you can't change your face

    G   F   G   F
But I see what you're made of what you gave up to keep me safe

G   F   G   F
Ah ah ah ah, ah ah ah ah ♥

    Em D C   Em   D   C
I keep breathing in, you make the rest of the world go dim

G   Em   C   G   Em   C
Your old friends say you're a monster but they don't know you like I know you

    Am   Am/B   C
You're fighting it, you're fighting it so hard

G   Em   C   G   Em   C
I don't mean to want you only but gravity is pulling on me

    Am   Am/B   C
I'm fighting it, I'm fighting it so hard... it's so hard

G   F   G   F
Ah ah ah ah (it's so hard) ah ah ah ah
G   F   G   F
Ah ah ah ah, ah ah ah ah   ♥

BUFFY + ANGEL
4EVA!!!

FOR THE VERSE +
THE LOVE THEME,
USE THESE VOICINGS:

      "G"   "F"
D —0——   —0——
A —2——   —3——
E —3——   —1——

* *FOR BONUS POINTS **
THERE ARE SOME HAMMER-ONS
AND PULL-OFFS THAT CAN
BE DISCERNED FROM
THE RECORDING!

USE THESE VOICINGS FOR THE CHORUS + PRECHORUS!

Em   G

D   C

Am   Am/B

Dead Man's Party

One thing that makes *Buffy* so special is the show's ability to seamlessly blend horror, hilarity, and the pulling of heartstrings. You're laughing! You're crying! You're scared! In "Dead Man's Party" there is very real, very serious personal conflict running throughout: Buffy has just returned home after disappearing for several months. In the moments after killing Angel to close the portal to hell, she hopped on a bus to Los Angeles—and told no one where she'd gone. Her mom and her friends are hurt and confused. But alongside the tension, there's also a mask that raises the dead, a zombie cat, and a delivery of empanadas from Joyce's new book club pal Pat. The episode culminates in a giant house party in Buffy's living room—including a surprise drop-in by dozens of the walking dead.[1]

We wanted this song to feel like an easy-breezy bop, so I used mostly major chords and deployed a laid-back strumming pattern and sunny *ba da da da ba*'s. But in honor of the underlying conflict between Buffy and company, I made the first two phrases of each chorus three bars long instead of the more predictable four, throwing the song slightly off balance just as Buffy tells us, "*I don't know what I'm supposed to do / Inside I just feel so black and blue.*" Then we find our way back to balance with a return to a four-bar phrase and her resignation to her circumstances: "*I'm not really in the party mood / but the zombies just got here and I don't wanna be rude.*"

---

1 Pat shares some schnapps with Joyce privately in the kitchen during the party, bringing a little bit of "will they/won't they" energy into the Summers household, before she herself is inducted into the undead club and subsequently killed with a shovel. RIP Pat.

3.02: DEAD MAN'S PARTY

INTRO: A D E A | A D E A

A   D   E   A
Mom brought home a mask, fresh from the gallery
A   D   E   A
I think is possessed but she thinks it's nice
A   D   E   A
All my friends are out cruisin the alleyways
A   D   E   A
Are they glad I'm back or they tellin lies?

KIBBLES
+
BITS
+
BRAINS

CHORUS!

E   D   A
I don't know what I'm supposed to do
E   D   A
Inside I just feel so black and blue
E   D   F#m
I'm not really in the party mood...
     E   D
But the zombies just got here and I don't wanna be rude

RE-INTRO: A D E A | A D E A

A   D   E   A
There's a zombie cat down with the dinner plates
A   D   E   A
And now neighbor Pat brought schnapps to share

F#m   D
Mom said they met at book club, seems legit to me!

A   D E   A
Willow's flippin out, Xander oughta shut his mouth
A   D   E   A
Giles found the key and hates Americans

< REPEAT CHORUS! >

A   D E   A
Coming home is hard, but it's where I belong
A   D   E   A
Oh hey here's a shovel - BLAM! it's in her eyes

F#m   D
Sorry mom I never wanted to kill your friend Pat

BLAM

A   D E   A   A   D E   A
BA DA DA DA DA BA BA BA DA BA DA BA DA DA DA DA BA BA BA DA

New Moon Rising

In "New Moon Rising" Willow reveals to Buffy that Tara—the girl with the zig-zag part from Wicca Club with whom she has been casting many a late-night spell—is more than just a friend. I have been on Willow's side of this coming-out experience many times over the years, so I am no stranger to the potential for anxiety in the lead-up and awkwardness in the aftermath. But we weren't writing this song from Willow's vantage point. Telling the story from Buffy's perspective began as a fun challenge . . . and ended up becoming a tender and affirming experience.

I am harder on myself than I would ever be on anyone else; I think this is true for many of us. At my most self-critical, I sometimes try to imagine how I'd respond if the roles were reversed: If someone I cared about were in my shoes, and I were in theirs, would I be so critical of them? Similarly, I needed to step into Buffy's shoes and consider what might have been going on in her head as she listened to Willow (her best friend!) share this new part of her life. The compassion and solidarity I was able to express in Buffy's voice served as an important reminder that we all deserve a friend who, no matter the circumstance, can pledge, "*Whatever your song, I'm singing along with you.*"

4.19: NEW MOON RISING

CAPO 5 (or play a guitalele...
or capo where you like!)

ALL CHORDS
RELATIVE
TO CAPO!

G   C   G G   C   Em
A shoebox hidden underneath your bed filled with parts of you you can't confess
     C   G   D   Am   D
This world was made to make you feel alone, but I'm forever in your corner, don't you know

CHORUS!

              C   D   G
Whatever your song I'm singing along with you
              C   D   G
Whatever your path I got your back, you know that I do
              C   D   G   D/F#   Em
Nothing that comes could ever divide us, you know I'll be right by your side
              C   D   G
Whatever your song I'm singing along with you

         G   C   G G   C   Em
If you think that I could ever judge you, let me break the gavel in two
     C   G   D   Am   D
This world will play you like a domino, but I'm forever in your corner, don't you know

HOPING THIS
CAT STRIKES
YOU AS 'MAGIC'

< REPEAT CHORUS! >

INTERLUDE: G G C G | G G C Em

Em   C   G
I can't imagine anyone holding up a candle to you
Em   C   G   D
And when I need somebody I know that you'll be there for me too

< REPEAT CHORUS! >

         G D/F# Em D C
With you   (REPETITION
         G D/F# Em D C   CAN BE AN
With you   IMPORTANT
         G D/F# Em D C   PART OF
With you   SONGWRITING!)
         G D/F# Em D C
With you

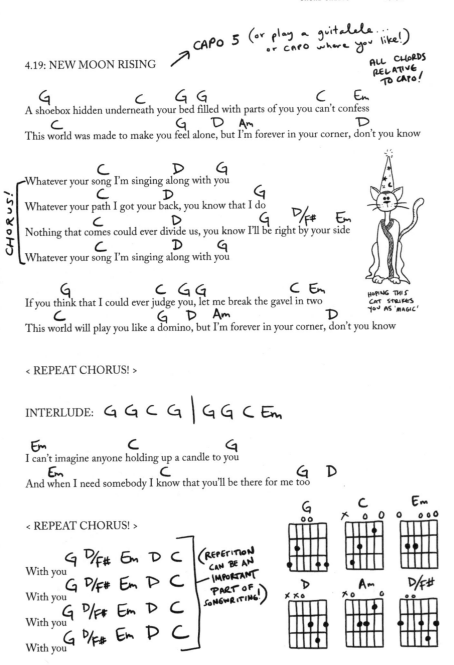

G   C   Em   D   Am   D/F#

Life Serial

Over the years, we were astounded again and again by the fact that in the vast institution of organized demon fighting, the Slayer—the one girl in all the world guaranteed to be risking life and all four limbs—is the only person *not* collecting a paycheck. The Watchers Council is a large and moneyed organization with numerous employees, many of them "potential" Watchers, training for a mantle they will never actually take up. How does this make sense?! PAY BUFFY SUMMERS, we often cried into the uncaring abyss!

This disturbing truth cuts deeper in "Life Serial" when Buffy is resurrected and discovers that while she was busy being dead, she also became . . . broke. The money left after her mother's passing has been eaten up by medical bills, utilities, and Dawn's general upkeep. On a downward existential spiral that is all too relatable, Buffy decides to have an IDGAF kind of night and goes out drinking with Spike, where she is introduced to his unfortunate habit of gambling for kittens.

This song was an opportunity to explore Buffy's financial woes—and the worst case of being underappreciated in the workplace that I've ever heard of—but we tried to match the episode's tone and keep it light.

In the instrumental break of the song, where usually I'd play a guitar solo or restate the melody on another instrument, I decided to pay homage to the adorable basket of poker kittens and instead recorded a choir of meows.

6.05: LIFE SERIAL

B
While I was buried way deep down six feet underneath the ground
A   **E**   **B**
Somehow I spent all the money that there was

B
Five months later I awoke, freshly un-dead, freshly broke
A   **E**   **B**
I wish money didn't matter but it does

                A   **E**   **B**
I've been working the late shift for a while
                A   **E**   **B**
I've been working the late shift with a smile
          A   **E**   **B**
I work the night away but I don't get paid for my time

          B
Four people living in my house but three of them ain't helping out
A   **E**   **B**
Turns out bills aren't magic and won't pay themselves

                B
I make swamp monsters go ker-plat in two pigtails and one hard hat
A   **E**   **B**
But fighting demons doesn't put food on the shelves

< REPEAT CHORUS! >

                A   **E**
When life tells me to ante up, I'll try some whiskey in my cup
B
Never thought that I'd end up backroom kitten-poker drunk

A   **E**   **B**
Meow meow meow meow meow meow meow meow meow meow meow meow
A   **E**   **B**
Meow meow meow meow meow meow meow meow meow meow meow meow

< REPEAT CHORUS! >
(BUT MAKE IT SAD
THIS TIME!)

PAY BUFFY SUMMERS!!

OK – there are only
3 chords in this song,
and let's voice them
like power chords:

B: A: E:

```
e |---------------------
B |---------------------
G |---------------9-----
D |---9------7------9----
A |---9------7------7----
E |---7------5-----------
```

really you
could just play
the root notes
(the lowest note in
each chord, which
shares its name with
the chord) ⎯⎯⎯
and play them
palm muted! Then
enlist a couple pals
to play piano +
electric guitar all
high and sparkly.
That would rip!
Your thumpy guitar
will be doubling
as the rhythm
section! Yay!

The Gift

While romantic torment could be considered the emotionally traumatic bread and butter of the show's storytelling, *Buffy* certainly traffics in other types of pain. In "The Gift," Buffy is faced with an apocalyptic crisis that can seemingly only be averted by the death of Dawn. But the Slayer—committed above all else to saving her sister—finds a loophole. She reasons that if Dawn's blood can close the world-threatening portal, and if the monks who made Dawn made her *from* Buffy, then her own blood should be an acceptable substitute. She takes the leap, both figuratively and literally, and her theory is proved correct. For the second time, Buffy dies saving the world.

One of the most powerful aspects of writing songs for the podcast has been consistently writing from the perspective of someone else—namely Buffy Summers. This practice helped me be more vulnerable as a songwriter. When I write my own songs, I sift through the most intimate details of my life and decide what I am comfortable sharing. When I write from Buffy's perspective, the full scope of the story (and all of the pain that goes with it) is already established, and refracts through me. When it came time to dive into Buffy's experience of telling her sister that she would do whatever it takes to protect her, I was overwhelmed by the intensity of the experience. This is the song in the *Buffering* catalog that is the most difficult for me to play without crying.

5.22: THE GIFT

Am G   C Am G   C F
I gave what I had to give, I gave you my only gift
   Am   G C F   Am G   C F
The easiest thing I ever did was let it go so you could live

This one just really means a lot.

    Em F Am   G
No prophecy could undo what has to be
Em F Am   G
You and me, built from our blood
      Em F
All these memories
  Am   G/B   C   F
Without you then who would make more

Hope you have better luck than me not crying when you play it!

Am G   C Am G   C F
I gave what I had to give, became what the world needed
    Am   G C   F Am   G C F
But the times before never felt quite like this, let go of your hand so you could live

    Em F Am   G
No prophecy could undo what has to be
Em F Am   G
You and me, built from our blood
     Em F
All these memories
Am   G/B   C
I need you to stay and make more

F C F
ooh … ooh

     Am   G/B
You won't miss graduation
  C
I won't have to miss my mom
Am   G
Just let me do this thing
C   F
Let me move on

    F   G   Am
To close up the dark til it's gone
    F   G
To close up the night before —

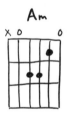

Am

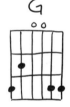

G

C

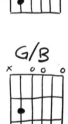

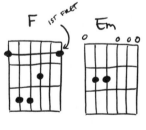

F 1st fret   Em   G/B

appendix d

THE BIRTHDAYS OF JENNIFER OWEN YOUNGS AS THEY RELATE TO THE AIRDATES OF BUFFY THE VAMPIRE SLAYER

Since somehow in the writing of this book Kristin's birthday has come up more times than Jenny's, it seems important that we properly balance the birthday scales.

During the run of *Buffering*, Jenny got into the habit of telling listeners the airdate of each episode and then doing the (Hell)math to explain exactly how far that airdate was from her next birthday milestone.

One of our listeners decided to take matters into their own hands and created a comprehensive grid for easier conversions.

EPISODES OF BUFFY THE VAMPIRE SLAYER IN RELATION
TO THE BIRTH OF ONE JENNY OWEN YOUNGS

SEASON 1	TITLE	AIR DATE	
Episode 1	Welcome to the Hell-mouth	3/10/97	only **257** days before Jenny turned 16
Episode 2	The Harvest	3/10/97	only **257** days before Jenny turned 16
Episode 3	Witch	3/17/1997	only **250** days before Jenny turned 16
Episode 4	Teacher's Pet	3/24/1997	only **243** days before Jenny turned 16
Episode 5	Never Kill a Boy on the First Date	3/31/1997	only **236** days before Jenny turned 16
Episode 6	The Pack	4/7/1997	only **229** days before Jenny turned 16
Episode 7	Angel	4/14/1997	only **222** days before Jenny turned 16
Episode 8	I, Robot . . . You, Jane	4/28/1997	only **208** days before Jenny turned 16
Episode 9	The Puppet Show	5/5/1997	only **201** days before Jenny turned 16
Episode 10	Nightmares	5/12/1997	only **194** days before Jenny turned 16

| Episode 11 | Out of Mind, Out of Sight | 5/19/1997 | only **187** days before Jenny turned 16 |
| Episode 12 | Prophecy Girl | 6/2/1997 | only **173** days before Jenny turned 16 |

SEASON 2	TITLE	AIR DATE	
Episode 1	When She Was Bad	9/15/1997	only **68** days before Jenny turned 16
Episode 2	Some Assembly Required	9/22/1997	only **61** days before Jenny turned 16
Episode 3	School Hard	9/29/1997	only **54** days before Jenny turned 16
Episode 4	Inca Mummy Girl	10/6/1997	only **47** days before Jenny turned 16
Episode 5	Reptile Boy	10/13/1997	only **40** days before Jenny turned 16
Episode 6	Halloween	10/27/1997	only **26** days before Jenny turned 16
Episode 7	Lie to Me	11/3/1997	only **19** days before Jenny turned 16
Episode 8	The Dark Age	11/10/1997	only **12** days before Jenny turned 16
Episode 9	What's My Line?: Part I	11/17/1997	only **5** days before Jenny turned 16

Episode 10	What's My Line?: Part II	11/24/1997	only **2** days after Jenny turned 16
Episode 11	Ted	12/8/1997	only **16** days after Jenny turned 16
Episode 12	Bad Eggs	1/12/1998	only **314** days before Jenny turned 17
Episode 13	Surprise	1/19/1998	only **307** days before Jenny turned 17
Episode 14	Innocence	1/20/1998	only **306** days before Jenny turned 17
Episode 15	Phases	1/27/1998	only **299** days before Jenny turned 17
Episode 16	Bewitched, Bothered and Bewildered	2/10/1998	only **285** days before Jenny turned 17
Episode 17	Passion	2/24/1998	only **271** days before Jenny turned 17
Episode 18	Killed by Death	3/3/1998	only **264** days before Jenny turned 17
Episode 19	I Only Have Eyes for You	4/28/1998	only **208** days before Jenny turned 17
Episode 20	Go Fish	5/5/1998	only **201** days before Jenny turned 17
Episode 21	Becoming: Part I	5/12/1998	only **194** days before Jenny turned 17
Episode 22	Becoming: Part II	5/19/1998	only **187** days before Jenny turned 17

SEASON 3	TITLE	AIRDATE	
Episode 1	Anne	9/29/1998	only **54** days before Jenny turned 17
Episode 2	Dead Man's Party	10/6/1998	only **47** days before Jenny turned 17
Episode 3	Faith, Hope & Trick	10/13/1998	only **40** days before Jenny turned 17
Episode 4	Beauty and the Beasts	10/20/1998	only **33** days before Jenny turned 17
Episode 5	Homecoming	11/3/1998	only **19** days before Jenny turned 17
Episode 6	Band Candy	11/10/1998	only **12** days before Jenny turned 17
Episode 7	Revelations	11/17/1998	only **5** days before Jenny turned 17
Episode 8	Lovers Walk	11/24/1998	only **2** days after Jenny turned 17.
Episode 9	The Wish	12/8/1998	only **16** days after Jenny turned 17
Episode 10	Amends	12/15/1998	only **23** days after Jenny turned 17
Episode 11	Gingerbread	1/12/1999	only **314** days before Jenny turned 18
Episode 12	Helpless	1/19/1999	only **307** days before Jenny turned 18
Episode 13	The Zeppo	1/26/1999	only **300** days before Jenny turned 18
Episode 14	Bad Girls	2/9/1999	only **286** days before Jenny turned 18
Episode 15	Consequences	2/16/1999	only **279** days before Jenny turned 18
Episode 16	Doppelgangland	2/23/1999	only **272** days before Jenny turned 18
Episode 17	Enemies	3/16/1999	only **251** days before Jenny turned 18

Episode 18	Earshot	9/21/1999	only **62** days before Jenny turned 18
Episode 19	Choices	5/4/1999	only **202** days before Jenny turned 18
Episode 20	The Prom	5/11/1999	only **195** days before Jenny turned 18
Episode 21	Graduation Day: Part I	5/18/1999	only **188** days before Jenny turned 18
Episode 22	Graduation Day: Part II	7/13/1999	only **132** days before Jenny turned 18

SEASON 4	TITLE	AIRDATE	
Episode 1	The Freshman	10/5/1999	only **48** days before Jenny turned 18
Episode 2	Living Conditions	10/12/1999	only **41** days before Jenny turned 18
Episode 3	The Harsh Light of Day	10/19/1999	only **34** days before Jenny turned 18
Episode 4	Fear, Itself	10/26/1999	only **27** days before Jenny turned 18
Episode 5	Beer Bad	11/2/1999	only **20** days before Jenny turned 18
Episode 6	Wild at Heart	11/9/1999	only **13** days before Jenny turned 18
Episode 7	The Initiative	11/16/1999	only **6** days before Jenny turned 18
Episode 8	Pangs	11/23/1999	only **1** day after Jenny turned 18
Episode 9	Something Blue	11/30/1999	only **8** days after Jenny turned 18
Episode 10	Hush	12/14/1999	only **22** days after Jenny turned 18
Episode 11	Doomed	1/18/2000	only **309** days before Jenny turned 19

Episode 12	A New Man	1/25/2000	only **302** days before Jenny turned 19
Episode 13	The I in Team	2/8/2000	only **288** days before Jenny turned 19
Episode 14	Goodbye Iowa	2/15/2000	only **281** days before Jenny turned 19
Episode 15	This Year's Girl	2/22/2000	only **274** days before Jenny turned 19
Episode 16	Who Are You?	2/29/2000	only **267** days before Jenny turned 19
Episode 17	Superstar	4/4/2000	only **232** days before Jenny turned 19
Episode 18	Where the Wild Things Are	4/25/2000	only **211** days before Jenny turned 19
Episode 19	New Moon Rising	5/2/2000	only **204** days before Jenny turned 19
Episode 20	The Yoko Factor	5/9/2000	only **197** days before Jenny turned 19
Episode 21	Primeval	5/16/2000	only **190** days before Jenny turned 19
Episode 22	Restless	5/23/2000	only **183** days before Jenny turned 19

SEASON 5	TITLE	AIRDATE	
Episode 1	Buffy vs. Dracula	9/26/2000	only **57** days before Jenny turned 19
Episode 2	Real Me	10/3/2000	only **50** days before Jenny turned 19
Episode 3	The Replacement	10/10/2000	only **43** days before Jenny turned 19
Episode 4	Out of My Mind	10/17/2000	only **36** days before Jenny turned 19
Episode 5	No Place Like Home	10/24/2000	only **29** days before Jenny turned 19

Episode 6	Family	11/7/2000	only **15** days before Jenny turned 19
Episode 7	Fool for Love	11/14/2000	only **8** days before Jenny turned 19
Episode 8	Shadow	11/21/2000	only **1** day before Jenny turned 19
Episode 9	Listening to Fear	11/28/2000	only **6** days after Jenny turned 19
Episode 10	Into the Woods	12/19/2000	only **27** days after Jenny turned 19
Episode 11	Triangle	1/9/2001	only **317** days before Jenny turned 20
Episode 12	Checkpoint	1/23/2001	only **303** days before Jenny turned 20
Episode 13	Blood Ties	2/6/2001	only **289** days before Jenny turned 20
Episode 14	Crush	2/13/2001	only **282** days before Jenny turned 20
Episode 15	I Was Made to Love You	2/20/2001	only **275** days before Jenny turned 20
Episode 16	The Body	2/27/2001	only **268** days before Jenny turned 20
Episode 17	Forever	4/17/2001	only **219** days before Jenny turned 20
Episode 18	Intervention	4/24/2001	only **212** days before Jenny turned 20
Episode 19	Tough Love	5/1/2001	only **205** days before Jenny turned 20
Episode 20	Spiral	5/8/2001	only **198** days before Jenny turned 20
Episode 21	The Weight of the World	5/15/2001	only **191** days before Jenny turned 20
Episode 22	The Gift	5/22/2001	only **184** days before Jenny turned 20

SEASON 6	TITLE	AIRDATE	
Episode 1	Bargaining: Part I	10/2/2001	only 51 days before Jenny turned 20
Episode 2	Bargaining: Part II	10/2/2001	only 51 days before Jenny turned 20
Episode 3	After Life	10/9/2001	only 44 days before Jenny turned 20
Episode 4	Flooded	10/16/2001	only 37 days before Jenny turned 20
Episode 5	Life Serial	10/23/2001	only 30 days before Jenny turned 20
Episode 6	All the Way	10/30/2001	only 23 days before Jenny turned 20
Episode 7	Once More, with Feeling	11/6/2001	only 16 days before Jenny turned 20
Episode 8	Tabula Rasa	11/13/2001	only 9 days before Jenny turned 20
Episode 9	Smashed	11/20/2001	only 2 days before Jenny turned 20
Episode 10	Wrecked	11/27/2001	only 5 days after Jenny turned 20
Episode 11	Gone	1/8/2002	only 318 days before Jenny turned 21
Episode 12	Doublemeat Palace	1/29/2002	only 297 days before Jenny turned 21
Episode 13	Dead Things	2/5/2002	only 290 days before Jenny turned 21
Episode 14	Older and Far Away	2/12/2002	only 283 days before Jenny turned 21
Episode 15	As You Were	2/26/2002	only 269 days before Jenny turned 21
Episode 16	Hell's Bells	3/5/2002	only 262 days before Jenny turned 21

Episode 17	Normal Again	3/12/2002	only **255** days before Jenny turned 21
Episode 18	Entropy	4/30/2002	only **206** days before Jenny turned 21
Episode 19	Seeing Red	5/7/2002	only **199** days before Jenny turned 21
Episode 20	Villains	5/14/2002	only **192** days before Jenny turned 21
Episode 21	Two to Go	5/21/2002	only **185** days before Jenny turned 21
Episode 22	Grave	5/21/2002	only **185** days before Jenny turned 21
SEASON 7	TITLE	AIRDATE	
Episode 1	Lessons	9/24/2002	only **59** days before Jenny turned 21
Episode 2	Beneath You	10/1/2002	only **52** days before Jenny turned 21
Episode 3	Same Time, Same Place	10/8/2002	only **45** days before Jenny turned 21
Episode 4	Help	10/15/2002	only **38** days before Jenny turned 21
Episode 5	Selfless	10/22/2002	only **31** days before Jenny turned 21
Episode 6	Him	11/5/2002	only **17** days before Jenny turned 21
Episode 7	Conversations with Dead People	11/12/2002	only **10** days before Jenny turned 21
Episode 8	Sleeper	11/19/2002	only **3** days before Jenny turned 21
Episode 9	Never Leave Me	11/26/2002	only **4** days after Jenny turned 21
Episode 10	Bring on the Night	12/17/2002	only **25** days after Jenny turned 21

Episode 11	Showtime	1/7/2003	only **319** days before Jenny turned 22
Episode 12	Potential	1/21/2003	only **305** days before Jenny turned 22
Episode 13	The Killer in Me	2/4/2003	only **291** days before Jenny turned 22
Episode 14	First Date	2/11/2003	only **284** days before Jenny turned 22
Episode 15	Get It Done	2/18/2003	only **277** days before Jenny turned 22
Episode 16	Storyteller	2/25/2003	only **270** days before Jenny turned 22
Episode 17	Lies My Parents Told Me	3/25/2003	only **242** days before Jenny turned 22
Episode 18	Dirty Girls	4/15/2003	only **221** days before Jenny turned 22
Episode 19	Empty Places	4/29/2003	only **207** days before Jenny turned 22
Episode 20	Touched	5/6/2003	only **200** days before Jenny turned 22
Episode 21	End of Days	5/13/2003	only **193** days before Jenny turned 22
Episode 22	Chosen	5/20/2003	only **186** days before Jenny turned 22

appendix e

BUFFERING THE VAMPIRE SLAYER'S SEXUAL TENSION AWARD WINNERS, BY SEASON

SEASON 1: CORDELIA + HERSELF (!!!)
in "The Puppet Show"

SEASON 2: SPIKE + DRUSILLA + ANGEL
in "I Only Have Eyes For You"

SEASON 3: ♡ BUFFY + FAITH ♡
in "Bad Girls"

SEASON 4: WILLOW + TARA
in "New Moon Rising"

SEASON 5: BUFFY + POWER
in "Checkpoint"

SEASON 6: GILES + ALL OF US
in "Two to Go"

SEASON 7: BUFFY + FAITH
in "End of Days"

AND THE ULTIMATE SEXUAL TENSION AWARD
(WANT-ALL) TAKE-ALL (HAVE-ALL) SERIES WINNER:

BUFFY + FAITH
in "Bad Girls"

THE END OF THE EPISODE

It's the end, it's the end of the episode
We've had some highs, we've had some lows
It's the end, it's the end of the episode
And everybody's lost now that they know

They can't see where to go
Or how on earth to get there
But they've made it up till now
And so

It's the end, it's the end of the episode
Guess we'll figure out together where we'll go

We've got lots of awards for tension to mail
Jingles to write and spoilers to veil
Hunks to examine, we'll manage somehow
Erotic novellas await, but for now . . .

It's the end, it's the end of the episode
And you know we hate to say goodbye
It's the end, it's the end of the episode
If you'll excuse me I have something in my eye

ACKNOWLEDGMENTS

This was an incredibly hard book to write. Emotionally, it is probably not advisable to sit in a room with your ex-wife and click—week by painful week—through your old shared Google calendar as you remember the way your life once looked. It is simply no fun to figure out how to put words and dates, images and anchors, to how that life fell apart. Kristin had a few panic attacks. Jenny developed sharp, stabbing pains in her jaw and shoulder. We would decompress by taking walks down to the local coffee shop or heating up leftovers for lunch while discussing the newest anti-aging face creams Kristin was using. Slowly and, in many moments, painfully, we pieced together the timeline that would become the skeleton for *Slayers*.

When you plot out your own history, time seems to shrink in on itself. We found new space for ourselves as we realized how quickly we'd moved through much of our heartbreak—we stared at each other in disbelief when our calendars showed that inside of three short days we'd announced a live show, released the first episode of a new season of the podcast, and published our divorce statement. We were shocked when we counted the actual span of days between Jenny's decision to leave our marriage and our standing onstage for our first *Buffy* Prom. We discovered a deeper appreciation for what we'd been able to accomplish, and for the many ways our community had held us together. Perhaps most impactfully, we started to see—for the first time—the path that led the way from that first, shattered life to where we now sat, still together, building what would come next.

Wherever Buffy, Giles, and the Scooby gang went after they walked away from the Gaping Crater Formerly Known as Sunnydale, things looked mighty different than they imagined on that first day of sophomore year at Sunnydale High. The same was true, as it always seems to be, for us.

We have so many people to thank for getting us from there to here.

Our amazing *Buffering* team over the years: Chase Alan, Brittany Ashley, Alba Daza, Sarah Duncan, LaToya Ferguson, Jim Grant, Lauren Klein, Morgan Lutich, Mackenzie Mac-Dade, John Mark Nelson, Devan Power, Zoe Regan, Josh Roth, Isabella Rotman, Sarah Stickle, Kristine Thune, Jennifer Vinci-guerra, and Laura Zak.

Our passionate editor, Lily Cronig, and the entire incredible team at St. Martin's Press, for believing in us and our story.

The wonderful humans who helped this book take its very first steps (and then some): Alyse Knorr, Gabrielle Korn, Diana Helmuth, and Tegan Quin.

The single best literary agent to ever agent literarily, Danielle Svetcov, who kept us inspired and alive during (and before, and after) the writing of this book.

Joanna Robinson, our anchor in the stormiest of seas.

Our friends and family—especially Riese Bernard, Lexy Casano-Antonellis, Randi Evans, Frank the Dog, Molly Green, Gus the Cat, Hrishikesh Hirway, Matty and Rey Luscombe-Daigle, Ingrid Michaelson, Matt Mira, Bess Rogers, Pete and

Rose Russo, the Singular Reverend Russo, Sam the Cat, Larry Youngs, Roxie and Greg Zak, and Helen Zaltzman—for cheering us on and holding us up.

Our current wives, Jess Abbott and Avanthi Govender, for putting up with us—a genuinely Herculean task (we couldn't even put up with each other!).

The cast, crew, and creators of *Buffy the Vampire Slayer*, for giving us a beloved story that begat a podcast that begat our most favorite community of all time.

The Scoobies who have kept us running in so many ways: world's best online moderators Rosemary, Jeremy, Kat, and Tort; The Two Emilys (one of Backpatches, one of Brackets); merch-slingers Alex and Jon; resident *Buffering* crafter LaRena; in-house carpenter and baker Scout; morale captain Stacie with her iconic Dancing Cat GIF; and *all* of our Scoobies not named here, the thousands of you who have made us us (and continue to do so).

And finally, we'd like to thank . . . each other. Sometimes after spending years making a podcast with someone, you look back and see only one set of footprints in the sand. Do not despair, for you were never abandoned. Look closer, and closer still, and you will see two pennies and a matchstick, which I dropped while I was carrying you.

SONGWRITING CREDITS

"Merry Go Round" written by Jenny Owen Youngs, Jacob At-
twooll, and Matt Zara. © 2018 Hipgnosis Notes / A Song
Can Be About Anything Music / Girls Raised By Wolves,
Bigger Picture Entertainment Global / Matt Zara Publishing,
Cooking Vinyl Publishing (ASCAP). Administered by Hip-
gnosis Songs Group, LLC.

ABOUT THE AUTHORS

Kristin Russo is a producer, speaker, and podcaster with a focus on LGBTQ issues. She has spoken at hundreds of universities nationwide, including Harvard, Stanford, and NYU, and has consulted with large-scale companies, such as Hyatt, Toyota, and Virgin Galactic, on diversity and inclusion. Kristin holds a master's degree in gender studies and is the coauthor of *This Is a Book for Parents of Gay Kids* and author of *A Quick & Easy Guide to Coming Out*. She lives in upstate New York with her wife and two cats.

Jenny Owen Youngs is a musician, songwriter, and podcaster. Her music has appeared in television shows including *Bojack Horseman, Grey's Anatomy,* and *Weeds*, and she has performed on hundreds of stages across the US and Europe. Jenny has also co-written songs recorded by Pitbull, Briston Maroney, Madi Diaz, and other artists, perhaps most notably the Panic! At The Disco multiplatinum hit "High Hopes." She lives in Maine with her wife, son, and Boston terrier.